PRAISE F(
The Well-Balanced World Changer

The Well-Balanced World Changer is a breath of fresh air for
leaders who need a crash course in the art of setting healthy
expectations and pushing through disappointment to stay
the course and finish well. This book is like a seasoned friend
who has the guts to tell you what you need to hear to push
forward in tough leadership territory. It provides dozens of
sticky insights that will help you pace yourself so you can live
out your passions and great ideas for the long haul.

—**BRAD LOMENICK, president and key visionary
of Catalyst, author of *The Catalyst Leader***

Change is hard. Keep going. Read this book and you will be
encouraged to pursue and balance your dream of changing
the world. We all need this.

—**JEFF SHINABARGER, author of *More or Less*,
founder of Plywood People**

Cunningham again reminds me that I am not a rock star
and neither are you. What a relief! Rather, we are more than
enough. Together we are God's hands and feet placed exactly
where he wants us for his purposes in our generation. Would-
be world changers get a fresh idea of what this looks like in an
ordinary yet intentional life.

—**SHAYNE MOORE, activist, author of *Refuse to
Do Nothing* and *Global Soccer Mom***

No one believes in your potential to change the world more than Sarah Cunningham. She's one of the most faith-filled and compassionate thought-leaders to come along in years. Yet her insights are grounded and her ideas will disrupt your long-standing beliefs. This is a must-read for anyone who dares to dream.

> —BEN ARMENT, creator of STORY and Dream Year

Reading *The Well-Balanced World Changer* is like having coffee with a good friend who cares enough to talk about things that really matter. You will feel exposed, challenged, and embraced all at the same time. This book is food for the soul of any world changer.

> —CHARLES LEE, CEO of Ideation and author of *Good Idea. Now What?*

The

WELL-BALANCED
WORLD CHANGER

The

WELL-BALANCED
WORLD CHANGER

A FIELD GUIDE FOR

STAYING
SANE

WHILE

DOING
GOOD

SARAH CUNNINGHAM

MOODY PUBLISHERS

CHICAGO

All Scripture quotations, unless otherwise indicated, are taken from the Holy Bible, New International Version®, NIV®. Copyright © 1973, 1978, 1984, 2011 by Biblica, Inc.™ Used by permission of Zondervan. All rights reserved worldwide. www.zondervan.com. The "NIV" and "New International Version" are trademarks registered in the United States Patent and Trademark Office by Biblica, Inc.™

Edited by Pam Pugh
Interior design: Ragont Design
Cover design: Connie Gabbert Design and Illustration
Cover image: Scale / Shutterstock

Library of Congress Cataloging-in-Publication Data

Cunningham, Sarah, 1978-
  The well-balanced world changer : a field guide for staying sane while doing good / Sarah Cunningham.
       pages cm
  Summary: "What happens when idealism and reality crash into each other (and you)? If you have ever passionately invested yourself in living your faith, championing a cause, or representing some noble ideal, you've probably experienced a faceoff between idealism and reality. This can lead to frustration, bitterness, disillusionment, loneliness, and exhaustion. Don't give in! This book is your survival guide. You can champion your cause and your faith, even in a broken and dysfunctional world. Stay in the race and take this guide along as source of fuel, rest, and encouragement along the way"—Provided by publisher.
  Includes bibliographical references.
  ISBN 978-0-8024-0766-5 (pbk.)
 1. Self-actualization (Psychology) I. Title.
  BF637.S4.C8596 2013
  158.1—dc23

We hope you enjoy this book from Moody Publishers. Our goal is to provide high-quality, thought-provoking books and products that connect truth to your real needs and challenges. For more information on other books and products written and produced from a biblical perspective, go to www.moodypublishers.com or write to:

Moody Publishers
820 N. LaSalle Boulevard
Chicago, IL 60610

1 3 5 7 9 10 8 6 4 2

Printed in the United States of America

To all of you who struggle against the world as it is,

In order to fight for the world that can be.

To those who wonder how you

are going to get through one more day,

Who sometimes feel like raising the white flag,

But who know, for the sake of good, that you need to keep going.

This book is for you.

CONTENTS

Never believe a few caring people can't change the world . . . that's all who ever have.

—MARGARET MEAD #worldchangerbook

WHY A FIELD GUIDE?

———— ✖ ————

Can I do it and stay sane?
Can I do it without my other priorities slipping?
Can I do it without neglecting the people I love?

—from page 62

Sometimes I wonder if life's greatest challenge is not *finding* your purpose in life, but *surviving* it.

That is why I've created what we're calling *a field guide for staying sane.* It's a map of collected wisdom for navigating the gnawing questions that threaten to sink the world's most passionate people:

How will I manage to keep up this pace long enough to make a difference? And if I do, what will I have sacrificed to get there?

To get any benefit from the content to come, then, it's important to first come to grips with this unfortunate truth. When you are intensely committed to a cause, when you invest your life in your beliefs and convictions for any sustained period of time, you will eventually—to some degree, at some point—encounter hardship. The causes you champion, no matter how pure or how noble, will not be immune to setback.

Even though nearly every human being on the planet is aware of the world's deficits—poverty, violence, oppression, apathy, anxiety, excess—society will not always welcome your ideas for improvement. The world will not always celebrate the rise of even the most brilliant, compassionate, or selfless people who seek to change it.

Moments of spiritual frustration too big to fathom will come when all of us will wring our hands and wonder at the mystery of a God who does not always intervene to clear the way on our behalf.

We will marvel at the endless lines of people in need, tremble at systemic issues so huge they seem un-dentable, and shed blood, sweat, and tears at the two-steps-forward, one-step-back progress that can leave us wounded and panting for breath from what seems like an always uphill battle.

In the meantime, our task is to learn to live well in the learning curve—to settle in and find a home in the tension between the way things are and the way we hope they will one day be.

We must recognize that being always busy, always tired, always emptied and dried-up creates an emotional poverty God never intended to birth or to hold our most cherished dreams.

Rather than abandon this drive or seek to subdue it, this book suggests wisdom improves every facet of life, every kind of personality, and every type of dream. It suggests that if we can acquire relevant principles and apply them to our circumstances, we can live smarter, love deeper, walk taller, stride more confidently, and enjoy more peace.

In making this claim, please know I don't present these ideas to you with any suggestion that I am a uniquely wise person. No one should give me a seat on the top of a mountain any time soon. In many, many cases, in fact, I prove quite the opposite. I have only stumbled onto wisdom after first failing miserably or making a variety of foolish or impulsive mistakes.

My hope, then, is you will enjoy and exercise more wisdom than I have and that the coming pages will save you a few bumps and bruises along the way so that you, like me, will wake up to fight another day. If you do and you want to tell me about the part of the world you aim to change, feel free to connect on Facebook (http://www.facebook.com/sarahcunninghampage) or Twitter (@sarahcunning). I'll even be inviting select readers to share great advice or wisdom they've acquired by guest-posting at my blog (http://www.sarahcunningham.org).

And as you're reading, if a quote jumps out to you that you think is worth sharing, whether it's a provided quote or one you draw out of a chapter yourself, we'd love it if you'd help us create a collection of online wisdom by posting it to your social networks using the hashtag #worldchangerbook.

Blessings on your journey, my fellow world changers.

Section 1
WORTH & SUCCESS

The world has not seen what God will do
through one man who is totally yielded to God.

—D. L. MOODY #worldchangerbook

THE BEST WAY TO BE PERCEIVED AS LEGITIMATE IS TO BE LEGITIMATE

THOSE WHO BRAG ABOUT THEIR IQ

———◆———

The elevator to success is out of order.
You'll have to use the stairs.

—JOE GIRARD #worldchangerbook

Is your soul swelling with a big, game-changing vision just begging to be adopted by the masses? Is the biggest want, or even need, of your cause or organization that you need exposure? That you need to be heard? be platformed? go viral?

Good for you for having something of substance worth sharing—for bringing something to the world, instead of just sucking the life out of it.

Now please take a number and hop in line.

Sound harsh?

It is.

But, sadly, so is the world.

If I had my choice, I'd give you a microphone. I'd set you up with national press conferences. Pay your way into the Super Bowl ad space. Get your stuff endorsed by A-list celebrities. Start a door-knocking campaign that made sure every resident in your area knew about the noble sort of things you're sinking your life into.

But I'm not the one in charge of doling out attention or platform in this world.

Here's the thing. As much as the average person might benefit from knowing about the causes we're fighting for, the movers and shakers in our field aren't going to line up around the block to listen to us. Random millionaires aren't going to take the initiative to show up at our door to bankroll us. Zuckerburg isn't going to personally champion our work to help us take the Internet by storm.

Instead, we're going to grapple. We're going to struggle to be heard. We'll have days when we feel like our voice is drowned out by a million others.

And when that happens—when you don't feel legitimized, when your work isn't validated, when people don't listen or seek to really understand what it is you're saying—you have two options.

The first is to wallow in the lack of resources available to you, to grieve the spotlight dancing just out of your reach, and to complain.

But here's another option worth considering.

Want to be seen as a leader in your field? Then get out there and *lead*.

Want to be perceived as being legitimate? Then, the best thing you can do is go out and *be legitimate*.

Not just for a day or a few months or for even a few years. But throw in, invest, show people you're in it for the long haul, that you're going to show up tomorrow, and next week and next month and the month after that. Be present, work hard, and prove you can be taken seriously as a long-term partner.

Asserting your own validity, especially when you're new on the scene, can make you seem like that socially inept intellectual you run into at a party. The one who tells you the exact results of their IQ test within 60 seconds of meeting them.

But be honest! You don't really want them to tell you they have an IQ of 180, do you? *You want to discover it.*

The same is true for ideas and causes.

It's like King Solomon said—In all toil there is profit, but mere talk tends only to poverty![1]

Is what you're doing as an entrepreneur, a writer, a speaker, a leader in an organization, worth hearing about? Then don't tell people it's worth hearing. Don't whine that people aren't listening. Don't go around telling people how you deserve a bigger platform. Prove you have some good ideas. Write them down. Talk about them with small groups. Serve someone already in leadership. Respect those who've gone before you.

The best way to be heard is to say something worth hearing.

The best way to go viral is to produce something worth sharing.

The best way to get attention is to do something worth noticing.

There is no blank check beyond that.

YOU'RE NOT GIVEN OPPORTUNITY, YOU EARN IT

SETH GODIN'S RED CARPET

—✕—

Some critics will write
"Maya Angelou is a natural writer,"
which is right after being a natural heart surgeon.

—MAYA ANGELOU #worldchangerbook

In my years as a high school teacher, I routinely came across students who weren't happy with the grade they received from me or another teacher.

"It's so stupid!" they would declare. "I can't believe she gave me a D."

And this is when I would give them the standard response that any teacher who hopes to survive must refer back to hundreds of times in any given year.

"Teachers don't *give* you grades, good or bad. You earn them."

Most of us can get a good smirk out of this one. Either we have an entitled child of our own or we can remember how entitled we were as children. But it's amazing, then, how quickly we sometimes forget this perspective as adults.

We see someone, Seth Godin, for example, who becomes a sought-after, nationally platformed speaker, whose expertise is quoted in thousands of newspapers, books, and blogs, whose books shoot to the top of the bestseller list. And we think, *Wow! The planet just hauled off and gave Seth Godin a world stage.*

And I know why we often get misled this way.

Some journalist, who by the way wasn't around all those late nights Seth Godin worked grueling hours trying to make something of his life, writes a snapshot story of the author's success.

Look what he did! He started giving away his book for free and then everyone wanted it. It catapulted him to dozens of bestsellers.

How simple success was for Seth Godin.

How nice of the world to just hand respect and notoriety over to him like that.

And we fall for it. We think, yes, yes one day—after barely working at all—Seth Godin was just leisurely sitting around on his porch sipping lemonade and an idea came to him. *I'll give my book away for free.* So the next day he did and he was suddenly on the cover of every magazine and his voice mail was full of messages from news producers.

How absolutely ridiculous of us! But how true, right?

The owner and editors of every major media outlet of his time didn't just show up on Seth Godin's doorstep and say, *We'd like to give you fame!*

He earned it.

Now true, our simple success stories have more lure. They're more fun to read. Easier to remember. Why? Because they suggest that maybe the same thing will happen for us. Maybe we will barely have to work at all and then one day the world will come knocking on our door to invite us to un-bridled fame and success!

A fun story, but we can't learn as much from it, can we?

If we really read all of Godin's blog posts, if we really read everything he's said in his speeches and TV appearances and magazine interviews, we'd get a completely different picture. We'd get a picture of a man who investigated the whole world, who ate, drank, and slept ideas, who read every book and article he could get his hands on, who learned from every person who crossed his path, who tried and tried and tried many times without world-recognized success.

Now, that is sort of disappointing, isn't it? So you do have to work hard for success.

But it's also freeing!

No one gave Seth Godin accomplishment. He earned it.

With that realization, you know exactly what to do. Stop hoping the next Seth Godin red carpet is going to roll down your driveway to your door. Get up and go earn your own grade in this world.

THEY DON'T HAVE THE AUTHORITY TO AFFIRM OR NOT AFFIRM US

THE DANGER OF LIVING OFF PEOPLE'S COMPLIMENTS

———————✖———————

I don't know the key to success,
but the key to failure is trying to please everybody.

—BILL COSBY #worldchangerbook

What good are fans?
You can't eat applause for breakfast.

—BOB DYLAN #worldchangerbook

The cheapest way to stir up good feelings for ourselves is to collect affirmation. Store up compliments. Let "nice sweater" or "great haircut" make us walk a little taller.

Remember nice things said about us, in person or online. Let "he's a brilliant thinker" or "she's a talented communicator" make us smile with satisfaction. Glean worth from applause, from awards, from promotions or recognition . . . from all those times someone notices how smart or efficient we are; what we've managed to pull off.

These kind of surfacey, impulse-driven good feelings are easy to come by. Post on Twitter or Facebook about having a bad day and three dozen people you knew in high school may come to your emotional rescue.

But things often come cheap because they *are* cheap.

Good feelings derived from affirmation too often unravel at the first sign of disapproval, say when someone mocks our new hairstyle or tells us our prized hipster glasses remind them of a celebrity we can't stand. They become sinkholes in our guts when we learn people thought we rambled on too long or went on too many tangents. They feed an ache to win people over in moments when no one claps, when the room falls silent, when others attack, interrupt, or dismiss us. They subtract from our emotional state on all the days when people don't notice what we're doing or how hard we're working; when people don't like or retweet us or read our blog posts in masses.

Affirmation, it turns out, is a short-lived and shaky refuge.

Depending on it allows the masses to influence our well-being, assigning commentators validity they probably have not earned and do not deserve. It unfairly lures our pool of acquaintances or online followers into a loop where they can skim off the top of us. Meanwhile, we wait for their reactions, reacting (and sometimes overreacting) to how they'll respond, egging them on to inappropriately appoint themselves judges who get to rate and score some one-dimensional expression of who we are.

The irony is they can clap or boo as loud as they want for the three-minute presentation you just gave, without ever really knowing the truly applause-worthy or disapproval-worthy parts of you. "Good talk" or "terrible blog post" is often a sadly detached critique from someone who doesn't really know the first thing about us.

I have come to believe Jesus would pull the carpet out

from under this equation, overturning our tendency to draw worth from this kind of empty critique. When the religious leaders of his time pulled this sort of thing, he wouldn't have it!

"How can you believe," he demanded, "since you accept glory from one another but do not seek the glory that comes from the only God?"[2]

Is it any different for us? How then can we, we who try to embody the way of Jesus in the modern world, claim to hold God so high and yet still put so much worth on the words of humans?

Addiction to approval can mess with us. It can actually prevent us from knowing and being known, allowing us to get our approval fix too easily and excusing others from bothering to understand us as filled-out, living, breathing human beings. As the people who dig deep for their kids, who persevere to grow through pain, who don't quit even when life gives them reason, who put in time reflecting and growing and becoming time and time again.

To present your fullest self in friendship and draw steadiness and strength from those around you, you often have to be willing to do something pretty tough: let go of the approval of the masses.

WHEN GOD IS INVOLVED, THE BACKUP PLAN CAN BECOME THE ORIGINAL

WHEN GOD WALKED THROUGH A COVENANT IN TWO FORMS

———————— ✖ ————————

Success consists of going from failure to failure without loss of enthusiasm.

—WINSTON CHURCHILL #worldchangerbook

I don't doubt God could lead a person to a specific place or a specific task.

I also don't doubt that if and when he prods us forward, we might—in our distractedness—miss his promptings altogether.

But here's what I do doubt: That we're supposed to be anxious about this, worrying about how we might've missed some destiny he pointed us to three years ago and now we're cursed to some lesser path.

I don't buy that God ascribes to that kind of do-or-die mentality.

Even if we miss some sort of cue along the way, I firmly believe God maintains an uninterrupted desire to bless us just as much as he would've had we been more attentive or responsive.

In our human economy, if we don't execute the ideal, the backup plan is usually lesser. It's the best and least taxing secondhand way to get something accomplished, given that we already missed the absolute best path.

It's more work, less rewarding, and may not produce an equally good outcome. But it's the best we've got.

Not God though.

God can insert the backup plan right over the original and weld them together. He can make this draft of the plan— forged from your successes and failures—so productive, so enriching, that it's as if the first plan never existed. Somehow your left turn takes you exactly to where a right turn would've taken you.

My Old Testament professor, Dr. Bailey, bolstered my confidence in this when he described the covenant Abraham entered into with God in Genesis 15.

Here's the CliffsNotes: In Jewish tradition, when two beings entered into an oath, they would split a sacrificial animal into two pieces and walk together between the two halves of the animal.

This was to signify the importance of their vow to each other. It was like saying, *If we don't fulfill our part of the bargain, then the blood of this animal is on our hands. If we fail to follow through, we shed its life for no reason. So break your promise and that abuse is on you.*

But when God made his covenant with Abraham, check out what happened in verse 17.

God appeared in two forms: smoke and fire. And those two forms passed through the two pieces of animals, while Abraham lay in deep sleep.

The Bible doesn't comment on why.

But given what we know about the tradition, it creates a powerful picture of redemptive backup plans.

God didn't have Abraham walk through the pieces alongside him. He didn't make Abraham vow to perfectly keep his covenant to God. Instead, he walked through in two forms, as if perhaps to illustrate that in his grace, and despite our failings, he would keep both parts of the covenant.

God would not only hold up his part of the covenant. But if and when Abraham missed the mark, God wasn't going to abandon his promises. He wouldn't throw down his oath and say, well, Abe, it's on you. You took a left when you promised to take a right.

No, he would still hold up his own part of the covenant.

And he'd guarantee Abraham's part of the covenant too.

He'd forge Abraham's backup plan right back into the original.

PROGRESS IS SOMETIMES TWO STEPS FORWARD

THE THINGS PETER NEVER GOT

———————✈———————

*A goal is not always meant to be reached,
it often serves simply as something to aim at.*

—BRUCE LEE #worldchangerbook

You're realizing it now, aren't you?

You've taken on something absolutely huge. And despite your best efforts, the results are a long way from what you had hoped.

You wanted to teach people new skills that reverse a lifetime of conditioning. You wanted to activate society around a cause that hadn't been on previous generations' radars. You wanted to inspire people to press into deeply knowing God and fully embodying his ideals.

But you've done all you can, put in all your energy, and you can't check a single completed task off the list.

Reality has not lined itself up with your specific, stated goals. People are still waltzing about making bad decisions, not always implementing the skills you've taught them. Society is still charging forward, only occasionally pledging some extra pennies to your cause. People are still clocking in and out of Sunday morning services, as if this single hour of programming and community is the end all, beat all of what spirituality has to offer them.

This is where the head bashing begins, right?

How could this be? we cry!

How could we lay everything on the line and show up day after day and still, so little is changed?

I have a feeling Jesus could relate.

Take Peter, for example.

He was the first guy in, the first guy called off the seashore. He spent all that time by Jesus' side, taking in teaching, handing out bread and fish, really absorbing Leadership 101.

But did he instantly take on the health and focus of Jesus? Not even close.

It was like his mind was a sieve. He let some things in, but a lot of things just seemed to flow right through him. In one ear and out the other.

He was always shooing the wrong person away, falling into the water, cutting off a soldier's ear. He was telling Jesus not to go to the cross, denying he even knew Jesus, hiding in a house—afraid and not knowing what to expect—even though Jesus had said he'd rise from the dead three days after he was crucified.

Peter, Peter, Peter! Jesus could've bashed his head against the nearest fishing boat. Weren't you standing there all that time? Didn't you hear what I said? Didn't you see what I did? What has all this been for?

But this, even in Peter's case, is not how progress works.

It does not arrive all at once.

It comes in bit by bit.

The urban high schoolers you work with may not graduate from high school and then college, they may not wait until they have jobs and own a home before they procreate, they may not become model citizens who don't even break the speed limit and may not become pastors or missionaries or small group leaders.

But here is what we must ask ourselves.

Are they better off than the day I met them? Do they know something more than they knew back then?

Did they pick up some wisdom about how to weigh two decisions and make the best one?

Did they begin to claim values—and stand for them—in their own ways?

Did any fruits of the Spirit surface?

We ask the same questions across the board, regardless of our context.

Do the people in our communities know more about a world issue we brought to them than they knew when we started? Are they more aware? Have they contributed to a cause in some way? Have they learned enough about it that they've started mentioning it to others? That they're talking about it online?

What about your church or faith community? Do they know more about Jesus than they did before? Do they now own a Bible? Have they read more of it than they had coming into it? Do they try to pray? Do they pray more? Do they exhibit more kindness, more self-control, purpose?

Are they two steps ahead of where they were?

Well yes, we say. Yes, but we wanted things to be so much different by now. We had bigger plans in mind than this!

That is fantastic you have spoken such big hopes over the

situation. That you've dreamed such full dreams over people's lives.

Perhaps in the short amount of time you've known them, with the resources you had, given the life circumstances they found themselves in, you have been exactly what they needed to get on that outlined path toward greatness. Or, perhaps, if they had already started on their way, you've given exactly the kind of support to keep them moving in the right direction.

You gave.

You contributed.

You encouraged.

It meant something.

Why would we be disappointed we didn't fully save them? That we didn't transform the entire situation altogether, in every way, shape, and form?

Why would we ever have expected that?

Why would we have ever thought that was our job in the first place?

We aren't the Savior in this narrative!

We aren't responsible for the outcome of other people's lives. We aren't responsible for the fate of the entire planet. We're just responsible for what we do with our stretch of time.

We don't have to get them across the finish line, we're just prompting things two steps closer to it.

Perhaps we need to look for the day Peter got the beginnings of what he needed to know to make his journey. For the moment he looked Jesus in the eye and got it right, "You are the Christ, the Son of the living God."

We have to look for those two steps forward and trust that even better things lie ahead in Peter's future.

GOOD MAY JUST BE YOUR NEMESIS

WE DON'T FIGHT GOOD

*Show me a thoroughly satisfied man
and I will show you a failure.*
—THOMAS EDISON #worldchangerbook

We've all got our definitions of good.

Whether it is what our parents would consider good—or what our culture might thrust upon us.

We've all got our benchmarks. What we'd consider "doing all right" by 25 or 30, 40 or 50. Maybe we determine we're doing okay by what kind of house we live in or what kind of luxuries we can afford, what kind of position we hold at work or what life accomplishments we've achieved, what kind of family or friend dynamics we have, how often we travel, how much time we have for entertainment or recreation.

Well, I'm unconventional, we cry.

I've never wanted what those people want.

I'm not some run-of-the-mill office dweller, you know.

I've got dreams.

Visions.

Causes.

But it doesn't matter.

We've got our ideas of good too. What's acceptable for

someone at our age, in our generation, in our region with our skill sets. Maybe it's working for a certain kind of company. Maybe it's being on the right rung in our climb up to lead pastor. Maybe it's doing some freelance work we love on top of our regular work.

So maybe we settle in when we get there.

Whew. We're not embarrassed by the makeup of our life. We're bringing in enough money to scrape by. We've got a job in the general industry we want to work in. Or we have a role using a skill set we are good at. Or we get to interact with people and we're people persons.

Home is okay. We don't spend quite as much quality time with a spouse as we wish we did. Or we don't always get the kids to sit down to dinner. We end up working many nights, but everyone has enough to eat and everyone knows they are loved.

Win-win, right?

But be so so careful.

Do you hear the benchmark you're using to assess your life?

Good? Fine? Satisfactory?

Really?

That sounds terrible!

Okay sounds like a terrible thing to measure life by. When you were little, did you grow up dreaming of having an average life? When people ask your children about their childhood, are you hoping they will say it was so-so? When your coworkers talk about you in retirement, would it please you if they stood on a stage and described you as average?

May no teacher ever force her class to watch a boring documentary of your life!

Is good really all that good? Are you constantly drawn to more? Do you have to have regular pep talks with yourself, building a case for why this stage is okay?

It's good. Really it is. Seriously, it's fine.

Maybe that's a sign that good isn't the exact right fit for you.

Maybe good is even your antagonist. It is your arch-enemy. Your biggest foil. Your nemesis.

My nemesis? we protest. *How can good be our nemesis? It's just good.*

Because it may be tricking you, that's why.

Standing there, disguised, blocking the path between you and your dreams.

And you just accept it. After all, everything is fine. What is there to argue or feel bad about?

See how good might steal your dreams without you even noticing? That's a talented nemesis indeed! To run off with your hopes and visions without you even realizing anything has been taken!

Now evil! You know to run from evil. If things were bad or harmful, you would get busy changing them. But when things are good, you're not afraid. When things are good, you're comfortable. When things are good, you can coast a little, reflect a little less, put dreams on hold until . . . never.

Maybe good is pulling the wool over your eyes. Enticing you to live the life you asked for instead of God's exceedingly more than you ever imagined.[3]

Maybe good is the very worst thing that ever happened to you!

GETTING ATTENTION IS NOT THE SAME THING AS BEING ADMIRABLE

EVEN CAR WRECKS TURN HEADS

———————— ✖ ————————

There is no logical reason why the camel of great art should pass through the needle of mob intelligence.

—REBECCA WEST #worldchangerbook

Anyone can grab a pot and a wooden spoon and stand out on the street clamoring for attention.

Go ahead. Set up a soapbox. Buy a spotlight. Sell tickets. Put on a show.

But just know, make sure you know down deep in the places where you hold all things important, that begging for attention is no virtue. Not on its own.

Your nonprofit got noticed. So what?

You're a regionally influential church now? Who cares?

You've become a sought-after speaker with a national tour? Big deal.

You're the "go-to" in your community, the one with all the programs, with the great music, with the people wearing jeans who welcome you as you are.

All of this is well and good, but by itself? Not all that impressive.

But we've got people on the edge of their seats, you protest. The world's eyes are locked on us. We're turning the heads of thousands . . .

We're the up-and-coming new guys. We're taking the stage in force, we're filling the speaker slots, grabbing the re-tweets. We've got fresh faces. Fresh ideas. Fresh movements. We've got a new model, an innovative start-up, a crisp conference idea right out of the oven. Our arsenal is packed with hot concerts, powerful CDs, popular books, flash-in-the-pan festivals. We're sweeping the hipsters en masse.

We're coming into our own. We're the talk of the spiritual town!

Applause. Autographs. Introductions. Fans and Followers . . . and *bam*. Celebrities are born! Brands are forged! Masses are gathered!

The world is standing at attention.

Yes, yes. And all of this can and very well may be used for great good. And you sincerely deserve some admiration for working so hard to get there.

But turning heads?

Please don't tell me that's how you measure success.

You're turning heads? So is the accident on the side of the road.

All kinds of things turn heads. A heap of mangled metal, blood-splattered windshields, engines caught on fire, over-turned semis.

People slow down. They gawk. They tweet about it and even take photos.

Crowds gather at a corner to watch an apartment building burn. They'll huddle on their porches as a neighbor is vis-ited by the police.

Do the people being observed—the offending drivers, the owners of the burning house, the resident being interrogated—think their observers are looking on in admiration? Do they suspect the crowds gathering up are their new fan clubs coming together?

Do the people in the accidents deserve medals? Should we give them some sort of prize? Is this something to be celebrated?

Of course not.

Getting someone's attention is not the same thing as creating a disciple. Turning heads isn't the same thing as gaining the allegiance of a long-term donor or board member. Screaming in the street isn't the same thing as being a loyal mentor or friend for the long run.

Fame! Notice! Recognition! Bah, humbug. What does the crowd know? The crowd gets fixated on anything shiny, turning their heads like a bird flocking to a piece of tinfoil.

The crowd looked at Jesus, the man who accepted the marginalized and spoke hope over the world, and picked Barabbas.

FAME IS NOT ALWAYS
THE GREATEST EXPRESSION
OF OUR GIFTS

MAYBE BILLY GRAHAM
WISHES HE WERE YOU

---

*Envy is the art of counting the other fellow's blessings
instead of your own.*

—HAROLD COFFIN #worldchangerbook

Do you hope to be huge? To be Rick Warren or Rob Bell or Billy Graham? To be Oprah, Angelina Jolie, or Blake Mycoskie (the guy behind TOMS shoes)?

Bill Gates, Steve Jobs, or Mark Zuckerburg? John Grisham, J. R. R. Tolkein, or C. S. Lewis?

Sheesh, I hope not.

What influential people. What example of human beings fixed on a goal. What examples of people whose work landed in front of millions!

But the world would be a pretty overstimulated place if there were thousands, even millions, of Billy Grahams. All competing over the stadium stages. Doing evangelistic crusades left and right—one for every day of the year, for every venue in the city, in every city in the world. It would take something away from it, wouldn't it?

Likewise for Steve Jobs. The world would be a very distracted place if there were thousands, even millions of him. All designing sleek, efficient gadgetry with great branding. Releasing a new product every time you blinked—one for every second of the day, for every day, for every year. It would take something away from it, wouldn't it?

So while there's no doubt that every Billy Graham and Steve Jobs of the world are good examples of some things—hard work or devotion, for instance—I'm not sure that necessarily means they're the best examples for you and me.

Who's to say they have reached the pinnacle of human experience? What it means to be Christian leaders or advocates or entrepreneurs? That they got the most privileged or blessed route of anyone in their era?

Maybe.

They certainly experienced favor.

But maybe, just maybe, being Billy Graham isn't the dream life. Maybe traveling from city to city, living out of a suitcase, seeing an ocean of new faces every night, each place blending in with the next, with no permanent community to invest in wouldn't be as luring as we think it would. Maybe there's something equally significant, even preferable, about being the man or woman who lives in regular community with people, side by side, alongside them, celebrating births, dedicating babies, baptizing, marrying, burying the dead— really knowing and investing in people over the course of life.

Maybe there are some gifts people at the local level get that Billy Graham can't touch. Like maybe Billy Graham would've loved to know where all the people who converted to the Christian faith at his events ended up. Maybe he'd have given his right arm to see them grow in their faith over months or years, to be able to support them to make sure they didn't feel isolated or unresourced, to watch them grow up or grow older and take on visions of their own firsthand.

Maybe (and there's a wealth of crash-and-burn A-listers to support this) it's not amazing to be famous, to be recognized. To not have people lobbying you to say things this way or that way. To think you have the answers to every political squabble or war. To have your privacy infringed on, to have everything you say be taken as representative of the entire Christian faith, to have every gadget you produce immediately met with knockoffs by your fierce competitors. Talk about pressure!

Maybe the freedom of being able to live out your faith and dreams and visions, in the good moments and in the bad moments, in some sort of privacy, at a more manageable scale, among people who know you is something cherishable.

Maybe the *Time* magazine People of the Year are the rich guys writing checks and you are the widow giving your two mites. Maybe in today's Jesus parables, you'd be the one who *really* got it right.

Maybe Billy Graham and Steve Jobs and Angelina Jolie wish they were you.

MAYBE YOU WON'T BE PRESIDENT

THE LITTLE LADY WHO MADE
4,000 STAND UP AND APPLAUD

Real success is not onstage, but offstage as a human being, and how you get along with your fellow man.

—SAMMY DAVIS JR. #worldchangerbook

Maybe you will not be the president of the United States who signs all kinds of important legislation into being. Maybe you will not even be a senator or congressional representative. Maybe you will never champion adoption reform, campaign for families, or create policy that builds up local communities.

Maybe you will not be the president's advisor or the CEO turned lobbyist who has breakfast with him. Maybe you will not even be some run-of-the-mill professor or lawyer who reads the story about the president via their subscription to the *New York Times*.

Maybe you will not even be the person who knows the person who is cousins with the guy who walks the president's dog.

Maybe you're not even on the nation's radar.

Maybe you will be the poorest of the poor, an impoverished soul who lives on the cheapest of diets with the sparsest of resources, who pours yourself out to others, who works with the least of the least, day after day for next to nothing.

Maybe it will look like your life is void of achievement, empty of applause.

Maybe you will just be that invisible set of hands and face, who is occasionally called upon to represent the religious or humanitarian communities. To go to the hospital when people are hurting. To comfort those who are grieving. To give little talks or prayers during annual ceremonies and conventions.

But you just never know.

None of us do.

Maybe, during one of those talks, you will pour out what you have seen in your work. Maybe you will plead with those present to stop aborting children, and instead, maybe you will find yourself volunteering boldly to take any unwanted child who is brought to you. Maybe you will vow to find every single one of them a place to be loved. To belong.

And maybe as you finish your little spiel and reassemble the pieces of your heart you've lain out on the stage, you will look out on the room and see, to the surprise of your younger self, that every person in attendance has risen to their feet to applaud you.

And that there standing among the applauders are 4,000 national leaders from both political parties, one of whom is the president of the United States.

Maybe it will be in this wise moment that you know that the only criteria that could've possibly gained you this platform and earned you the favor of these usually divided people, is the fact that while everyone else was getting applause, earning votes, and creating media buzz, you got yourself something more powerful than all of that.

Credibility.

Maybe you think this is a ridiculous claim and a fantastical story. That sure, in the Bible, and theoretically, it's the Samaritan who makes the right choice, not the religious official.[4] It's the person who got their hands dirty in prison or gave the needy water who did right by Jesus.[5] But the good guy doesn't win; that is not real life. That is not modern-day reality, a voice inside us may protest.

I think that too sometimes.

But maybe before either of us land firmly in that conclusion, we should take a good long look at what happened on February 5th, 1994, at the National Prayer Breakfast in Washington D.C.[6]

Section 2
HEALTH & BALANCE

Every great dream begins with a dreamer.

—HARRIET TUBMAN #worldchangerbook

HAPPINESS IS NOT SYNONYMOUS WITH YOUR GOAL

IS ANYONE ELSE DOING THE SAME THING YOU ARE, BUT HAPPILY?

———————◄►———————

Happiness is not a goal; it is a by-product.
—ELEANOR ROOSEVELT #worldchangerbook

What's the wonderful thing about goals? They can consume you.

What's the terrible thing about goals? They can consume you.

It's incredible if you are so devoted to your goal that you hold to it, clinging to it over the mountains and through the valleys, carrying it along through thick and thin, rocks and pastures.

As you trudge uphill, against opposition and disbelievers, dodging bullets, in the back of your mind—your goal, your mission, informs you. It beats along with your heart, *I must stop oppression. I must find a way to meet these needs. I must get the funding. I must, I must, I must.*

These mantras push us forward in adversity, inspiring us, allowing us to reach new depths and heights.

But then one day, the goal changes . . . ever so slightly. So slightly we might not notice it.

We tack on one smaller addendum.

It's just one little phrase pasted onto our goal. But that one little phrase can be deadly.

It goes something like this:

I'll only be happy if . . . I am able to stop oppression.

I'll never be satisfied unless . . . I am able to meet these objectives.

I cannot find contentment without . . . securing X amount of funding.

I can only feel gratified if . . . my blog gets X hits or X comments a day.

Do you see what happens to us there? Slowly, unintentionally, we begin to identify our goal with contentment and a happy life.

We cannot feel contented when we are not progressing in our cause . . . at the rate we wish to progress.

And this is when goals tend to get sticky.

Because then we reprogram ourselves to think that in raising our cause, we are striving toward happiness and contentment. But really this is just an illusion.

Yes, your goal is probably going to bring about good for many others and make you feel good. But is your goal or life mission *really* the same as happiness? We must realize as soon as possible that it isn't.

A book of teachings collected from Anthony DeMello helped me conclude that happiness and contentment are a lot broader than that.

Can you experience happiness away from your goal? DeMello might ask.

When you are away from your cause and holding a newborn child or grandchild? When you're laughing with an old friend? When you're hushed before a beautiful landscape? When you're vacationing away from it all, can you experience happiness?

Well then, if we can experience happiness without our goals, then our goals are not happiness.

Or what about this: Do others, others who have nothing to do with your particular goal, experience happiness or contentment? Is anyone, anywhere doing something completely different than you, but still happy?

Well, the same holds true then, doesn't it? If others can experience happiness or contentment apart from our goals, then our goals are not happiness . . . not in and of themselves.

It sounds trivial. Like something we already know. But coming to grips with it, really internalizing it, is a revelation. Learning! Growth! Ah-ha!

It opens our minds!

We can suddenly release goals, or parts of goals, or ways of looking at goals that we need to abandon.

Maybe we were so convinced happiness was caught up in our goal that we were unable to tweak it the way we needed to. Maybe our current way of funding our goal isn't the right way after all. Maybe the way we're spreading our message isn't exactly the right appeal. Maybe our pacing, our schedule, our workload . . . maybe something is off. Maybe it's always been off. But because we refused to consider a life apart from this one particular way of achieving our goal, because we were afraid of wrecking our path to contentment, we locked in on something bad.

Maybe our goal, when implemented the wrong way, when it consumes us and costs us and makes us adopt unhealthy patterns, is so obviously *not* happiness. Maybe, in fact, it's the source of much of our *unhappiness*. And maybe it also stirs unhappiness in others—neglected family and so forth.

And please let's not create exceptions for ourselves.

Let's not try to get away with saying, *Well, I've really thought this through and my way is really the only way to achieve this goal. And doing it is just hard and it's not an easy or happy road to getting there.*

Really? Are you telling me there is no one, no one who has ever lived or who is living now, who is approaching your same goal but is able to manage their emotions to allow them to experience happiness now . . . along the way . . . before happiness is reached?

Someone, somewhere isn't bogged down by the same things you are. But because their wiring, their approach, their way of prioritizing is different than you, they're able to take a go at a big mission and yet still experience happiness.

Let's take this one step further. Don't we, as persons of faith, believe that goodness, well-being, peace, fulfillment are found in Christ? Of course we do! And do we think that somehow God is withholding happiness, that he refuses to let us experience good in the time being, that he will only let us be happy on the day we finally meet our goal?

What a terrible God that would be to serve! Why would anyone serve a God like that?

The apostle Paul was one of those annoying wise and opinionated people who had perspective. He was the guy who went fiercely after the goal, but could still be happy. He said in every situation, he could be content.[1]

That's because Paul and other visionaries realize

something: they realize their goal is not synonymous with happiness.

So that frees them to be happy even while they're pursuing it.

People have told you a lot of things about what God wants for you. He wants you to spread his good news? To care for the poor and the oppressed? To love others, even your enemies?

Yes, yes, all of that, yes!

But he also wants us to experience fullness. To be content. To be well! Go ahead. I dare you to believe in a God who has not strapped a burden on your back to prevent your happiness. I challenge you to believe in a God, who among many other missional, purposeful things he'd like for you, who—right now and not just someday—wants you to BE HAPPY.

PLANT YOURSELF.
HOLD FIRM AND GIVE OFF LIGHT

BE A LIGHTHOUSE

The martyr sacrifices themselves entirely in vain . . . for they make the selfish more selfish, the lazy more lazy . . .

—FLORENCE NIGHTINGALE #worldchangerbook

Many of us are taught, starting in childhood, to never, *ever* give up.

It applies even more so to those of us in the nonprofit, charitable, and faith arenas. We often work with hurting, broken but incredibly valuable people. We want to be the sort of inspirers who those we love and serve will one day be grateful for. And about us, we hope they'll say, "When everyone else threw in the towel, *this person* never gave up! She was always there for me. He never quit no matter how many times I messed up or tried his patience."

If this is how you think, good for you. That is very noble.

But you've got to stop running around after people and cleaning up their messes or they will never get to that place. They will never say that about you.

You know what I'm talking about, don't you? I'm talking about that fine line between being a persevering supporter of a person and being an enabler of bad behavior or poor choices. The line between being dependable and creating someone who is dependent on you.

There's a place for both. But to choose awareness, we must ask ourselves, *If, at the end of trying to help someone, I am depleted, spent, and dried up, has anyone really been helped?*

Who has been helped?

If they or their problems had you running in circles, pacing up all night, taking you away from your own life priorities, have you been helped? If other people in your life who rightfully deserve your attention—family, friends—have been neglected as you chased after others, have they been helped? And if they are not yet ready to benefit from your help and continue to make poor choices time and time again, well then, they have not really been helped either.

Something important may have been said. Some kindness that matters may have been shown. Seeds were planted, good was done, all is not lost. But help has not yet been accomplished.

So what is a committed person to do?

We certainly can't justify abandoning the person, washing our hands of their failures and walking away.

Could we perhaps tell them to get back to us if they get to a place where they really want our support in the future?

Why not?

What if that was the very best thing we could do?

What if we, like my friend Glenn House once told my friends and me, saw ourselves as lighthouses? Or as Jesus put it, a city on a hill?[2]

What if we saw ourselves as beacons of light, promoting goodness and purpose and truth in this world? And when we shine, we help other people orient themselves as well. They see our light and it gives them direction. They better know where they are and where they need to go.

But does a lighthouse pull itself out of the ground and chase after ships in the water who ignore it? Does it go in circles, following reckless captains to make sure they never hit a rock or capsize?

No!

If it did, it would reduce its service to everyone. A lighthouse helps orient people. Its steady presence gives people a sense of where they are. *Ahhhh. There's the shore.* If it were always uprooting itself, it would lose its very specific purpose.

Lighthouses plant themselves in a community and give off light. And all who want to benefit from their light are welcome to.

But if someone decides they'd like to go off pontooning in murky, choppy waters, damaging their vessel the whole way?

The lighthouse just keeps standing there, shining.

We can do this too. Plant ourselves in our communities and make our purposes and commitments clear. We can reach out to those in need, express interest in supporting their well-being. But we don't have to frazzle ourselves chasing them in circles. Instead, we shine light strong and steady. And when they go through their cycles and pass by us again, we keep shining light. We persevere to shine it on them every time they pass. And eventually, when they are ready and tired of darkness, they may very well come to a place where the light starts to look good and they're more interested in staying in a sunnier, healthier, happier place.

And then what? Well then, thank God, we will still have energy left to be of service!

ENDLESS LINES OF NEED

THE POOL OF BETHESDA

———————◆———————

*God has put within our lives meanings and
possibilities that quite outrun the limits of mortality.*
—HARRY EMERSON FOSDICK #worldchangerbook

The problem with being an idealist . . . well, there's a lot of
problems. You've figured that out by now, haven't you?

But one of them is that it takes a long time—*your whole
life long and then some*—to make a dent in some needs.

Some causes are gigantic. To raise your charge, to champion those you advocate for, can be a mammoth undertaking.

If you feed a homeless man some soup, what do you find?

You have one homeless man who is fed. This is good and
right and pleasing to God.

But what comes next?

Another homeless man.

And a homeless woman.

And three more homeless people after that.

You feed them all soup. And Jesus' heart is warmed. It
is as if you gave soup to Jesus himself, Matthew 25 suggests.

But is homelessness stamped out? Are the problems of
affordable housing, economic disparity, or inequitable wel-
fare policies resolved?

Of course not. Soup is beautiful, soup is a gesture of love, the flesh and touch of a caring Savior.

But soup is also just soup. It doesn't reverse government policy, it doesn't erase generations of injustice or right economic structures. It doesn't impart truth from every noodle or carrot in a spoonful.

So what happens? Word spreads.

And now instead of five homeless people, there are fifty-five.

Well, you scoff, I'm giving them more than soup! I'm giving them friendship, care, I'm helping them in finding work, shelter, and a support system.

Of course you are! And I'm so glad you're doing that.

But if you rally every agency in town and get all fifty-five of those homeless friends into homes, if you find fifty-five places of employment, and fifty-five counseling support systems, is homelessness wiped from the face of the earth?

Of course not!

What happens if you feed—and create a loving community for those fifty-five? Well, they come back with fifty-five new friends.

But what if you *really* organize? What if you pull together every social service under the sun, what if you call in favors with every care worker or mission director you know? What if you find a place—not just a home but a rooted position in society—for every person in your city?

Well then, I admire you. And your life is well spent.

But homelessness, you already realize, will not have been eradicated.

Because the next city over has homeless people too,

doesn't it? And the one beyond that. And even if you re-create your efforts in each one of those, stamping out homelessness one city at a time, this big old flawed world works against you.

Brand-new people in your home city, and in those first cities, will fall into homelessness. They will lose jobs, become refugees, get divorced. The breadwinners of their families will die. And some of the people you helped get out of homelessness will find themselves without homes again too.

Someone will take advantage of them. Some landlord will turn them out. They will quit a job they don't like only to find there are not many jobs available to replace it. Or they will lack the life skills to keep up with their newfound responsibilities.

Do you see what I'm trying to point out to you? It sounds depressing and downright discouraging at first, right?

But be of good cheer.

Even Jesus' purpose was not to right every need in existence or stamp out every harmful systemic issue of society.

And that kind of offends us.

You might be thinking, but what about Luke 4? What about when Jesus tells people that he's been feeding the poor and healing the sick? And that this shows the prophecies of a messiah are fulfilled in him?

It's true.

Thank God in heaven, it's true.

How much easier it is to be endeared to an accessible, compassionate Savior than a begrudging angry God who seems apathetic to human suffering!

But think about the pool of Bethesda.

When I was in college, I heard an urban leader speak about the pool of Bethesda.

What really happened about the pool of Bethesda? he asked.

Well, it was this fabulous pool, everyone tells him. A place where sick and injured gathered, because every great once in a while, an angel would come and stir the water and whoever touched the water first after it was stirred would be healed.

And when Jesus went to the pool, how many people does the Bible record that he healed? the speaker asked.

Well . . . we scramble into our memories of Sunday school lessons, looking up the verse in our Bibles.

One.

One person! Why did Jesus heal only one person at the infamous pool of Bethesda where the poor gathered?

The leader, who was no uncompassionate person himself as he invested decades of life fighting poverty and crime in the inner city, suggests it is because Jesus' mission was not to stamp out every need on the planet . . . or even on his continent . . . or in his town.

Even Jesus, if we notice, did not spend himself chasing after every person in need he could find. He did not launch about cities, yelling out, *Poor people, please come to me, so I can find you jobs. Hungry people, come out of your houses, so I can feed you!* He did not go around knocking on doors, saying, *Do you have any sick people here? Do you know anyone who lacks food? Money?*

This is sometimes crazy to think. We almost want to argue it, but Jesus just didn't carry on this way, did he?

Even he, he who is God and who came to save the world in ways we cannot, even he did not wipe out every need in every place.

What did he do? He stuck to his purpose. He'd come to give life—a spiritual life of living water, bread of heaven, fullness, a new way of living that upturned society's values and called people to love their enemies and care for the poor. And he went about doing this, speaking about it, sharing it, day in and day out.

Now that is not to say Jesus did not help or heal people. To say that would be a sticky, terrible sort of heresy!

When someone in need crossed Jesus' path, he absolutely met the need.

When the blind called out to him, he made them see.

When the man who couldn't walk was lowered through the roof as Jesus was teaching, he made him walk.

But even the God turned man who came to save the world, the only one who really could do it, even he didn't run himself ragged, driving himself into the ground chasing after every need.

Jesus went about his mission, spoke about a better way, and called everyone who heard him to embrace that better way. And when he ran into people who needed help, he helped them.

Perhaps we would be better off if we took up his example.

JUST BECAUSE YOU CAN DO IT, DOESN'T NECESSARILY MAKE IT THE BEST CHOICE

IT'S NOT WHAT YOU CAN DO, BUT WHAT YOU CAN DO HEALTHILY

The difference between stupidity and genius is that genius has its limits.

—ALBERT EINSTEIN #worldchangerbook

I was born with a dangerous disposition.

When I attempt something new, especially if it is something I believe in, it rarely even crosses my mind that I will fail.

It's not that I think I'm invincible. Or that I'm a genius. I know I'm not.

It's not that I think I would be the fastest to figure it out. In fact, depending on the challenge at hand, I am well aware it may take me a great deal longer than other people to accomplish.

It's not that I think I won't fail along the way. Most of the time I expect to fail . . . multiple times. And it's not that I think that I'm a natural who is suited for everything, who can excel to be the best who ever lived. I know that is not true.

No. It's that I tend to think that I have enough capability

and determination that, if given enough time, I could figure out just about any challenge I believed was important to solve. *Eventually.*

That's great, some of you say. What a blessing. Stop bragging!

No, what is great is that in saying this you are choosing to see the positive in me. But unfortunately, those of you who are like me know that this kind of reckless ambition and unboundaried willpower can lure us into some sketchy situations.

Here's what I mean.

We world changers get an idea.

Maybe it's a vision we want to see brought to fruition or a cause we want to see taken up.

It seems impossible. Inhuman. Outside of what is practical.

Only a flaming, raging idealist would take such a crazy task on. Hence, why we are first in line.

Those people who are busy naysaying and insisting there is no way it could be done? The opportunity to prove them wrong only bolsters our confidence!

Can I do it? we ask. And then we assess it. We mentally list all the task will take. We calculate carefully. We break huge tasks into smaller parts. We create an internal timeline of how we will knock it out, one day at a time.

And we conclude we can. And in many, if not most cases, we are right.

But here is the problem. In assessing the task, we have asked the wrong question. Just ever so slightly.

We should not have asked, Can I do it? We should've asked, Can I do it healthily?

Can I do it and stay sane?

Can I do it without my other priorities slipping?

Can I do it without neglecting the people I love?

This is an altogether different question.

Of course, if we ask the question without any qualifiers, we might be able to do it. If we can sideline everything else in our lives. If we can stay up until 3 a.m. every night working late into the night. If we can eat crackers or bananas or any food that comes fast and allows us to stay glued to our computer. If we take our laptop to the pool and a stack of papers to the couch or the bleachers, where we pretend to participate in family life.

And when we ask the more appropriate question, we find it often impacts our answer.

Can I do it? Yes.

Can I do it and stay healthy? Probably not.

There is no pride in being able to do something at the expense of everything and everyone else. This doesn't make you superman, it makes you foolish! But does it make you smarter or stronger or better than the next guy? No! Maybe a lot of other people could do it too. They're just not dumb or selfish enough to try.

Just because we *can* do it doesn't make it sane or healthy.

And just because we *could* pull it off doesn't necessarily make it right.

ERR ON THE SIDE OF HEALTH

HOW TO INTERACT
WITH A HUNGRY TIGER

—✖—

Let the fear of a danger be a spur to prevent it;
he that fears not, gives advantage to danger.
—BENJAMIN DISRAELI #worldchangerbook

A person who becomes a parent often develops a deeper appreciation for safety and a heightened radar for danger.

Boil water on the back burner, turn pot handles in. Lock away razors. Move chemicals to nonaccessible places. Relocate the block of kitchen knives to the back corner of the counter.

There is no messing around. When in doubt about whether some object poses a danger to the kids, the kids win and the object loses. We don't want convenience or easy access nearly as much as we want our children's well-being.

It is cut-and-dried.

We not only distance them from all known threats, we even avoid the possibilities of threat. We err on the side of health.

What is amazing, then, is that we can so easily understand this concept as it relates to our loved little ones and still sometimes neglect the same kind of care and watchful eye for ourselves.

We toy with our own well-being. Bet our integrity a little more often. Put our health on the line. Walk out on a few limbs.

We feed an addiction.

We cheat to get ahead.

We overeat and underexercise.

We text and drive.

We start gambling.

We flirt with a married coworker.

We do things that put our lives or the quality of our lives in jeopardy.

If you could take us out of the situation and ask us objectively to give someone else advice about these dangers, we'd come up with all the right answers. But somehow when it comes to ourselves, we allow a little more room for sloppiness or selfishness.

Why? This makes no sense.

What if we came upon a hungry tiger lounging in the middle of the room? A force we knew could rip us apart, immobilize us, paralyze us, end us.

Would we creep up on it? Tiptoe as close as we could get, as quietly as we could, without waking it up?

Would we reach out and touch its fur, gently, softly, out of curiosity for how it might feel?

Would we lift up its paws or pull back its lip to reveal claws or teeth up close?

Of course not! We'd make a mad exit, slam the door, and head for the hills.

So why is it that we tempt failure? That we'll get as close to compromise, as close to losing as we can instead of running from something dangerous? That we pretend the tiger is a domesticated cat that won't hurt us if we pet it?

We have to put on our parent mind sometimes. Place ourselves in the shoes of God our Father. Someone who is sane, unaffected by our impulses and emotions. Someone who wants long-term good for us and not failure.

And we have to see the tiger for what it is.

A dangerous force with the ferocious ability to tear our lives or the quality of our lives into pieces. To harm us and to harm those we love. To destroy what we've spent so long building. To undermine our accomplishments, fill us with shame and steal our peace.

It's only when we see the tiger for what it is that we find the clarity and the speed and the will to do what is necessary when we come upon that fierce, hungry tiger: Get as far away as we can as fast as we can and never go back. Hold on to what is good and reject any kind of evil![3]

KNOW YOUR TRIGGERS

REVERSE PHILIPPIANS

———— ✖ ————

There are times when fear is good. It must keep its watchful place at the heart's controls.
—AESCHYLUS #worldchangerbook

I bet some people have sacred, inspiring ways for noticing imbalance in their lives. Perhaps during their breathing exercises or as they commune with God while perched on a rock out in nature, their soul senses some sort of disharmony.

My version is a whole lot quirkier than that.

Do you know what tells me there is some sort of imbalance in my life? It's when

my car gets really messy, but I haven't bothered to clean it
laundry piles up in our utility room
toilets go uncleaned
I go eight weeks instead of four between haircuts
I don't file or paint my nails
I screen almost all of my calls out
I make up excuses not to go to social events
I don't respond to emails
I have no idea what is happening on my favorite TV shows
I haven't read the newspaper in a week
I fall asleep in my clothes

I drink too much caffeine

I skip a meal or substitute fast food for something
nutritious

I don't make the time to run or do sit-ups

my tolerance is low

I miss people's cues or don't notice their needs

I don't spend enough time praying or reading or
reflecting

I don't make the effort to seek guidance or ask for help

It's the thousand seemingly little things that, when combined, keep my life together, that keep me sane and healthy and living in the moment.

It's when my life plays out as the opposite of Philippians 4. It's when I'm not rejoicing always, but I'm complaining always. It's when my *un*reasonableness is known to everyone. It's when I'm anxious about everything, even the things that are illogical to be anxious about. It's when I fail to pray and submit my request to God. And it's when I cannot sense the peace of God sweeping over my heart.[4]

I have to be careful because some of these things are small enough that they can fall almost unnoticeably. And by the time the domino effect is in play, and they are careening into each other, snowballing down a hill, it's hard to reverse the bad momentum before it topples my whole being.

Each one of us would be wise to identify the triggers that fire our unhealthiness. Because once we name them, we are more likely to notice them falling. And once we notice them falling, we are more likely to do something to stop it.

RECOGNIZE THE GATEWAY TO UNHEALTHINESS

KNOWING WHICH DOOR THE TIGER IS BEHIND

✖

Physical infidelity is the signal, the notice given, that all fidelities are undermined.

—KATHERINE ANNE PORTER #worldchangerbook

Pretty much nobody sets out to be a monster from day one.

A little girl does not declare that she hopes to make her children hate her one day when she is a mother.

A groom does not stand at the altar and plot how he will cheat on his wife.

A college student does not slave away on a plan to develop a reputation for being selfish.

We give human beings too much credit to think we're as calculated and intentional as all that.

Then how do we get there? How do we end up failing?

It's not that we don't grasp the big, orienting values—that we want to be a good parent, a faithful spouse, and a person of integrity. It's that we haven't taken the time or energy to identify the gateway behaviors that might lead to these ends.

We don't think about what slipping would look like.

What actions would help reverse that drift away from our values?

Or what barriers might we put in the way of failure?

So when we find ourselves in the moment, in a place where we are tempted to depart from our values, we unexpectedly stumble upon a gateway. And we have to make a decision on the fly.

We have to rely on our instincts, hoping we can keep emotions and lust and social gratification at bay.

But that approach doesn't give us the best possible chance to make the best possible decision, does it?

If we want to make good decisions, decisions that support our intended values, then we have to expect opportunities to fail.

We have to name the steps that might lead to failure. We have to describe what the gateways to hurt look like.

As a mother, it might be giving in to our desire to control or interfere. It might be being overly critical. It might be justifying when we display reckless emotions, telling ourselves it is okay because our kids can separate out our bad days from our good. It might be insisting to ourselves the kids will realize that the real us they saw in so many good days is unselfish, supportive, and stable and forget all about the other behaviors they witnessed. It might be hoping they will somehow be immune to any bad feelings about those poor choices.

As a husband, it might be communicating with another person at work more than we communicate with our wives. It might be giving our best energy outside of the house, sharing our good moods and patience with those we spend our days with and bringing home the worst to our families. It might be increasing contact between us and some other woman, contact we may pass off as appropriate but that we still for some reason delete off our phones or email accounts. It might be looking in the mirror and hoping the woman at the office will notice how attractive we look or inventing reasons to pop in and say hi to her over and over and over.

As a person of integrity, it might be always noting some unfairness or flawed behavior on the part of another and always having it on hand to share. It might be rehearsing the flaws of some party who got on your bad side over and over and over again. It might be dismissing reasonable boundaries or moral hitches to put all the dirty details out there for family or other confidants. It might be finding some combatant, some reason to be bitter toward someone, in every organization, school, church, or group of friends you're a part of.

Can you name the possible steps that might lead you to destruction? For your sake, I hope so!

Now plan out what you are going to do when those gateways come into your field of vision.

What can you do to hold yourself accountable? To check the condition of your heart? To put a barrier between you and failure? To uphold healthiness?

When you can recognize the gateways to unhealthy living and you have a plan about how to avoid them, it will not make you impervious to temptation or immune to failure. But it will help, don't you think?

Remember that hungry tiger we talked about earlier? If someone told you that hungry tiger was behind a red door with a silver knocker on it, I bet you would stand a pretty good chance of never getting eaten by that tiger.

Section 3
PEACE & PERSEVERANCE

No matter what people tell you,
words and ideas can change the world.

—ROBIN WILLIAMS #worldchangerbook

HOW TO GIVE A LIFE

GIVE ONE DAY AND
THEN THE DAY AFTER THAT

———————————✖———————————

Here is a test to find whether your mission on
Earth is finished: If you're alive, it isn't.

—RICHARD BACH #worldchangerbook

As I've considered the popular subject of giving our lives to God, I've been reflecting on some of the ways belief is often prompted.

As a hand held up in a quiet service, a prayer repeated, a date of conversion scrolled in cursive on a flyleaf of a Bible.

All of this is well and good, of course. And it is all part of my story too. I chose my path on a particular day, in a particular moment—albeit a moment that followed a childhood of spiritual moments. A series of moments is hard to separate from the more conscious, verbalized decision day.

In addition to this, also like many, I have pledged myself to various causes—signing on to support faith communities, nonprofit organizations, and other worthy visions.

But I have something to say about these touted first moments of conversion, a more practical point than theological.

You do not give an entire life in a moment.

Yes, yes. I know. Theologically you do. Spiritually, belief has a beginning, a setting of a new track, a change of allegiance.

But what we give on that day, tangibly speaking, in terms of actual "time spent" is . . . well, *that day*. What we give in the moment we pray, is . . . *that moment*. Our alignment with God is determined, but how we spend the rest of our days that will make up this thing called life is still yet to be seen.

The same is true of many other passions. When we sign on to a new job, launch a brand-new nonprofit, donate our time to relief work, we pledge ourselves that day. But whether we attach ongoing energy to them, whether we make a long-term showing of support, is yet to be seen.

A lot of us in the religious world have figured out how to give God one moment. We celebrate this moment where our feet first find themselves on a new track.

Fire insurance. Eternal security. Bravo. Good for us.

Truly, we begin tasting new life!

And a lot of us have also figured out how to sign on to other causes. We know how to give a killer interview, pitch a book, launch an organization.

But to be credible, these "one moment" beginnings must find their expression in another all-important moment: the moment right after our alarm clocks ring every morning.

Somewhere between opening our eyes and brushing our teeth, our soul finds its calibration, its temperament for the new day. And we settle in, face the rising sun, give thanks to God, and figure out somehow, in all our defects, how to give the coming day to God and the causes he stirs in us. And then, despite the frustrations and the challenges and the temptation to give up, we'll manage to do the same thing tomorrow.

And if we give God the next day, the next day, and the day after that, eventually the days will turn into weeks. And the weeks will become months. And the months will accumulate into years.

Years will of course then give way to decades that fall one after another.

That is how we give a life. That is how, looking back, at all of those consecutive and ordinary days, we will *know* that we didn't just verbalize intentions but that we poured out our very lives for his purposes.

THE NEXT BILLY GRAHAM

GOD'S EYES SEARCH FOR
ONE WHO IS FOCUSED ON HIM

———————◆———————

Opportunity dances with those on the floor.

—ANONYMOUS #worldchangerbook

While we're talking about giving a life, there's something else I want to say.

Your life is just as good as the next guy's.

Really.

So maybe when you were younger (or yesterday for that matter), you heard a story about someone who was "born to change the world" or "destined to make their mark." Maybe you heard some revered Christian leader, some standout entrepreneur, some notable philanthropist described as "anointed."

And maybe so.

I certainly don't disclaim God's ability to lock someone into a specific vision or equip them in supernatural ways should he want to do so. But my gut says that these kinds of tellings are only half of the story.

Does God stir some vision inside of them? Does he put them on a path where they stumble onto opportunities that advance that vision? Sure thing. Does he bless their efforts? No doubt.

But when we attach mythology around notable people, acting as if the hand of God distributed fill-in-the-blank famous writer's books to the masses, I think we leave out some valuable data.

Do we really think angels descended from heaven and unrolled a red carpet at the doors of the maternity ward where Billy Graham or D. L. Moody or C. S. Lewis were born? That invisible light beams shot down from heaven bestowing them with extraordinary powers?

Because if so, I worry that narrative lets a lot of otherwise talented people off the hook. That we've excused all those who haven't had a burning-bush calling from investing our abilities as much as we could. If that's what God wanted, he'd anoint us in an obvious way, right?

But consider this with me. What if the truth is that every one of us has the same anointing as Billy Graham?

This possibility occurred to me in elementary school as I read bios of notable leaders. Time and time again, the leaders had uncanny things in common. They had great conviction, they were often bold to a fault, they took risks, they put everything they had into their causes, and they were committed over the course of their entire lives.

I think it's possible that because these individuals felt stirred to effect some sort of good, they went all in. With sometimes reckless abandon, they decided who they were going to be, what they were going to stand for, and then they made thousands of investments—of time, money, energy—in their mission, which eventually paid off.

And I think it's possible that you and I could do the same thing. I don't assume what God stirs in Billy Graham will express itself in our lives in the exact same ways. But I believe the feeling of alignment, the desire to abandon ourselves to a cause, the fierce satisfaction of being in the right place at the right time, that those gifts may belong to all of us.

Let me ask you this.

What if you took that thing—that vision, that idea, that cause you believe has been stirring in your life—and you decided that you were going to do all you could to bring it to expression? Let's say you have ten or twenty or even thirty or more years of life left should you live a natural life span. Could you not make a dent in the cause you care about with that much time?

Or let me put it another way.

If you put twenty, thirty, or forty years into any end, giving yourself to it day after day, year after year, wouldn't it be hard *not* to make an impact?

If you wrote a vision statement today and began sharing it with people. If you wrote a book this year and began distributing it. If you championed a charitable cause this month and began raising funds. If you did these things long enough, if you kept showing up again and again, kept speaking your faith to person after person, don't you think eventually your work would spread?

What if Graham's platform had less to do with some special intervening selection on the part of God and more to do with Graham making himself available?

What if it had more to do with what is suggested three times in the Old Testament: The eyes of the Lord range throughout the earth to strengthen those whose hearts are fully committed to him.[1]

BE READY FOR THE LONG RACE

WINNING A SPRINT AND
FINDING OUT IT'S A MARATHON

---

*The vision of a champion is bent over,
drenched in sweat, at the point of exhaustion,
when nobody else is looking.*

—MIA HAMM #worldchangerbook

You may be a bit of a visionary. I bet you are. Good for you.

And probably, if you're the kind of person who picked up this book to begin with, you are also the kind of person who wants to get things done. To follow through. To not just put visions on paper but to execute them.

Your faith, your cause, burn red-hot in your heart. And it gives you the drive to get up early and face the day, to run through obstacles, to take on monsters.

You're willing to put in the energy and clock the hours to train, practice, be ready.

That's admirable. That kind of vitality and dedication is a gift.

But here is my worry for all of us in the faith, all of us who cleave to causes and raise our banners high.

We prep.

We train like crazy.

We're the runners of the ministry world, the sprinters of

the humanitarian field. We buy all the right gear, the running pants, the cleats, the sweatbands. We adopt the right diet— we bulk up on energy foods and cut out the heavy stuff. We wake up at the crack of dawn to race back and forth across the gym at lightning speed. We practice shooting off the blocks. We rehearse leaning in to the finish line. We clock ourselves over and over again until our times are competitive. We master the hundred-yard dash.

Then comes our time to shine.

On launch day, we feel great! We're in the center of the field, doing stretches while our playlist pounds through our earbuds.

We're jogging in place to keep loose.

Then we lock into our lane of the race, position our feet on the blocks, and when the start gun fires, we leap into long, confident strides. Our form is beautiful, our feet rhythmically connect with the ground, we are one with the track. We break away from the pack, the crowd cheers in awe. We make 50 yards, then 75, coming up to the 100-yard line . . . we're about to win . . .

And then we realize, to our horror, that it's not a sprint. It's a marathon.

The hundred-yard mark is just an early hashmark before many to come. The course stretches out into laps and laps.

We start to panic. We can't even see the finish line. Exhaustion creeps in. Our pace slows. Our sides ache with pain. We're jogging now, slowly devolving into labored breathing, cramps, and muscle tightness. Sweat pours down our face until we run out of sweat. We need water . . . we need water . . . we need water. There's no end in sight.

Tragedy!

I've seen this far too many times, haven't you?

People who are deeply invested, who have worked like dogs, who have read everything there is to read and learned everything there is to learn, who have lived and breathed and slept their mission. Who knew how to shoot out of the gates, grab everyone's attention, snatch up the limelight with the latest book, the latest conference, the latest cause.

They fire off the blocks, but once they realize there will be no immediate payoff, when there is no standing ovation, no medal or gold cup, no sense of completion, all too many times crash and burn in going the distance.

But this, this moment of dawning awareness, this instance when we realize just how big of a mission we've taken on, just how much race is still out in front of us, just how much our task is going to demand of us? This is where we must take hold of ourselves.

Where we must be prepared to interrupt whining, shoo away bitterness, oust pessimism. Give ourselves a good shaking, a slap across the cheeks, a cup of water in the face.

When we look ahead, and project drudgery and misery on all the laps left still ahead of us, of course those laps are going to be discouraging. When we declare unfairness over the length of the course, naturally we're going to feel defeated.

But what if—we see that the length of the course *is* the gift?

What if the fact that the track is long *is* what will save us?

What if we *need* every inch of the mileage ahead of us to succeed?

What if it is a gift that if you miss something on this lap, that you can catch it when you circle back around? What if it is a relief that if you lack a skill today, you still have time to build it and use it tomorrow?

We must never lock on to the hundred-yard dash illusion. We cannot afford such short vision.

Those who have long vision pace themselves. They look for rest marks along the way. They nourish their bodies every so many miles. They save themselves for the final stretch to give everything they have one last time.

You will not adequately prepare for the race in front of you, if you do not stop to recognize now what kind of race you are running.

Love the sprints, but train for the marathon.

WHATEVER YOU DO, KEEP GOING

DON'T RUN OFF THE TRACK

———————— ✕ ————————

It's always too early to quit.

—NORMAN VINCENT PEALE #worldchangerbook

You may wonder why I've been hitting these running analogies to death.

When I was in high school, I was a long distance runner. By national standards, I was nowhere near being ranked among top runners, but in my own little niche, one year, I was awarded the MVP for my contribution to the team.

I remember someone on the team who ran sprints, yards instead of miles, asking, "What is your mental approach? What are you thinking as you run laps and laps around the track?"

I had no idea how to answer.

"Do you think, *I have to catch the person in front of me*?" she guessed.

I thought for a minute about how aiming to catch the person in front of me did sound like a solid strategy. Just trying to take one person at a time. Focus on catching them, then passing them, and then locking on to the next guy.

That would probably work.

But that was not my answer.

What did I think about when I circled the track for the sixth time?

"I think *Don't run off the track*," I confessed. I think, no matter what, no matter how tired you get, no matter how much you want to quit, no matter how lush and green the grass of the infield looks, no matter how wet and quenching that water bottle on the sidelines appears, no matter what, don't run off the track. Just don't run off the track.

Sometimes the secret to success isn't figuring out things particularly well or having a secret, no-fail strategy. Sometimes it's just not quitting. On projects, in mission, in those difficult relationships.

It's just never allowing yourself to take your ball and go home.

Never hoisting the white flag.

Never forming the words, "I quit."

It's choosing not to send the resignation letter you've written in your mind.

It's jogging on the days you're too tired to run. And walking on the days you can't even manage a jog. And, should there be a day when you cannot walk, it's determining to crawl.

But unfortunately, I'm not done yet. It will get worse.

There will be days you cannot even crawl.

And even on those days, you must find a way to press on. You must sit and rest, while locking your eyes forward. And if you collapse in exhaustion, lying there on the floor, too drained and empty to even keep yourself upright, then stretch your arm forward and reach for the prize with everything you have left.

Want to be a great runner? There are a million ways to become one. You'll figure it out for yourself. Just don't run off the track.

TAKE THE TIME
TO REGULARLY CALIBRATE

MENTAL TRICKS OF
PEOPLE WITH LASER FOCUS

---

*The successful warrior is
the average man with laser focus.*

—BRUCE LEE #worldchangerbook

So you are going to persevere, I am going to persevere, we all are going to persevere. After all, none of us are quitters!

So all the quitters—the 32 percent of church planters that go under during their first four years,[2] the three out of four start-up businesses that fail,[3] and the roughly 30,000 to 60,000 nonprofits that disappear from the IRS's files each year for unspecified reasons[4]—where do they come from?

The obvious answer, of course, is the quitters come from people who don't start out intending to quit!

No one launches a new church, a new ministry, or a new nonprofit planning to be sidelined by difficulty.

So what is the difference maker? What separates the visionaries who don't intend to quit but end up throwing in the towel from the visionaries who maybe want to quit at some point, but who manage to stick it through?

The marketplace is full of data on the wide range of traits successful leaders and businesses share. But here's one observation that seems significant to me. You can decide whether you might buy into it too.

I propose to you that an important habit of standout leaders is their sometimes extreme commitment to calibrating over and over again. Calibration, of course, being that weird process you have to go through with your phone screen or computer monitor or printer where you make sure things are aligned correctly, that it is displaying the right color and brightness and so forth, so that you can trust the images you are seeing are accurate.

Over time, gadgets lose their clarity. They decrease in accuracy. So in order to function at their maximum, they have to be periodically recalibrated.

In the printer world, that sometimes means users must find a specially designed test image, which they can use to compare to what their printer is printing to see if the printer is producing the appropriate results. The literal meaning of calibration, then, is just "to check" or "adjust"; to compare against a standard.[5]

And I'm telling you all the best leaders do it.

An evangelist once said that every day when he walked out on his porch, he took a moment of intentional pause and imagined his front yard and neighborhood and all he could see as a battlefield. He pictured it marked by the sight of wounded soldiers and dead bodies. And then he considered how he would live if he believed everyone he knew was both physically and spiritually dying.

See, I told you visionaries' commitment to recalibration is extreme!

But you see how he was doing the same thing we do with

our printers more or less, right? His imagined picture of himself reacting to a battlefield was his test image. It was what he compared his life against in order to try to live his values most accurately.

Here's another one. One evening, evangelist D. L. Moody untypically closed a church service without giving an invitation—a time for people to indicate their desire to follow Christ or to heed some other sort of call on their life. That night, the great Chicago Fire broke out and some of the people who had attended his earlier church service died in the tragedy. Moody called his neglect to issue a call for people to follow Christ the biggest mistake of his life. And as a result, he always intentionally carried this mental snapshot of what it felt like to know people had unexpectedly passed beyond life into eternity with him into every church service. Whenever he stood onstage or at a pulpit, he purposefully recalibrated himself to the sincerity of that picture and let it prompt him to speak out of passion to welcome people to follow after God.

Again. Pretty extreme.

But this isn't just a habit of crazy or standout evangelists. It's a habit of some of the most successful business leaders as well.

Take Steve Jobs, for example, who while giving the commencement at Stanford, recounted some of his daily habits. "For the past thirty-three years, I have looked in the mirror every morning and asked myself: 'If today were the last day of my life, would I want to do what I am about to do today?' And whenever the answer has been 'no' for too many days in a row, I know I need to change something.

"Remembering that I'll be dead soon is the most important

tool I've ever encountered to help me make big choices in life." He went on to say, "Because almost everything—all external expectations, all pride, all fear of embarrassment or failure—these things just fall away in the face of death, leaving only what is truly important."[6]

Or take Reggie Joiner, one of the founders of Orange,[7] an organization that spearheads conferences, events, and entire ministry strategies for children and students. One day, after realizing how quickly life seemed to pass him by, Reggie calculated how many weeks he would live if he was able to reach the average life span for a male born in his generation. Then he placed a piece of rice in a bowl for each week he was projected to have left. Using this as a visual aid, he decided that at the end of each week he would force himself to go to the bowl and remove one piece of rice. This process of removing rice forced him to confront the fact that he did not have forever, that every day he was moving closer to an end of this life, and that he wanted to use the remaining days and weeks for good.

And this isn't just a habit of the famous.

My dad, who is also a pastor, has found a similar moment of calibration in something all of us could share. Whenever he hears an ambulance or fire engine siren, in addition to praying for whoever has fallen into tragedy and is in need of rescue, he makes a mental note to consider that alarm to be a warning. He intentionally pauses to remember that people around him every day are meeting with injury and death, that no life lasts forever, and that life can end suddenly and unexpectedly and allows this to influence his own actions and focus for the day.

Life. Death. Death vs. life!

Why all this talk about death? Why so consumed with the morbid?

Maybe it seems that way.

But I think if we look closely, we'll find that what these people are actually concerned with is life. Just as every printer or monitor will eventually cease to work, calibration is not meant as a painful reminder of their inevitable end. It's meant as a tool to keep them functioning as well as possible for as long as possible.

Calibration is about life! It's about living life well.

Calibration is the stuff of Israel. It's the setting up of twelve stones at the Jordan to remind their tribe of what God had done for them,[8] it's the tying of symbols on their hands and foreheads and writing Scriptures on the doorposts and gates.[9] It's about setting up moments of calibration that invite us into awareness, that invite us to stay focused, to become the people who may sometimes feel like quitting, but who remind themselves of what is important too often to throw up a white flag.

HOW DO YOU
DO IT ALL AT ONCE?

THE JUGGLER ALWAYS
SETS SOME THINGS DOWN

———————◆———————

Like it or not, the world evolves.
Priorities change and so do you.

—MARILU HENNER #worldchangerbook

I've had a strangely eccentric and varied life.

Among other things, I went to college and to grad school, lived at a homeless shelter, worked at a church, got married, made some lifelong friends, led a disaster relief team to Ground Zero, taught at-risk high schoolers, wrote five books, helped organize several conferences, and had two children.

It sounds like a lot when I type it all out like that, especially when I string it all together in one clean sentence linked by commas.

But don't be misled the way some of my readers or acquaintances have been.

"How do you juggle so much so easily? How do you do it all?" mothers often ask, imagining that my house is HGTV-worthy, that I cook like Rachael Ray, and that I homeschool my brood of twelve children all while saving Gotham City from criminals.

"I don't," I tell them.

And it's true. I don't do it all.

Even though I have done all the things in that one jam-packed sentence above, I didn't juggle them all at the same time. I didn't do them all in a year or two. I did them over the course of sixteen years. And often, I did them one or two or three at a time.

If you must compare me to a juggler, then you must put my act into slow motion and watch what I'm really doing. Because I'm not simultaneously juggling twelve different objects. All twelve objects might very well get juggled at one point or another, somewhere between the beginning and end of the routine, but here's the thing: I juggle a few, and then while I'm still juggling—just like you've seen many performers and illusionists do—I set one thing down and pick another one up.

Maybe it's hard to see because all you can remember is all the things you saw flying through the air, but if you watch close, there again! I set something else down and picked something else up.

Everything has a season.

If I'm writing, I don't teach a small group at church.

If I'm pregnant, I completely eliminate speaking from my schedule.

When it's crunch time in event land or I'm trying to make a deadline, my friends see less of me for a stretch.

Instead of shopping or knitting or reading style magazines or religiously watching certain TV shows, I write. That's my thing.

Truly, to everything there is a season![10] And did I mention that in some of those seasons, I ask for help?

When I was pregnant (and was trying to write), I paid a nice lady to come to my house and clean a couple times when we could afford it.

When I had a toddler and an infant (and was trying to write), I saved up some money to hire a babysitter for nine full school days and two half-days to watch my children while I typed in another room.

So when it comes to your belief that I or anyone else is effortlessly juggling a million things without dropping any? I'm afraid I must break it to you gently: there are good performers, but there are no real-life superheroes.

But that is actually a good thing. Because it frees all of us to be humans and only take on what we can handle without losing our sanity.

TYRANNY OF THE OUTWARD

CHOOSING PRIORITIES BASED
ON WHAT THE WORLD WILL SEE

Tear a man out of his outward circumstances;
and what he then is; that only is he.

—JOHANN G. SEUME #worldchangerbook

It's easy to check off the small stuff.

It's way easier, for example, to surf around Facebook liking pics and sharing pithy quotes, than it is to get out a puzzle or finger paints or a football and invest some serious quality time in the nearest kid.

It's easier to wipe down the counter, sweep the foyer, polish a mirror, than it is to call up a roofer, take a day off work, and figure out how to pay for an increasingly leaky roof.

It's easier to sit on a couch and watch reruns or sports or reality TV than it is to pick up a pen and write the first page of the bestseller inside you.

We want that feeling of completion. Something got done!

That feeling of rest and relaxation where we didn't have to expend a lot of energy.

That illusion of productivity where we at least occupied time. We stayed busy.

But this easy quick stuff, according to the landmark book *Tyranny of the Urgent*, is often what crowds out or diminishes our energy. We end up getting to the end of the day having done a million little things—straightened a bookshelf, returned a call, browsed some decorating ideas, read up on which celebrity wore it worst, checked Facebook five times—and barely anything of importance.

I'll add to that one other important tyranny to avoid.

The tyranny of the *outward*.

That decision to focus on what people will see—some career accomplishment, a blog, a book, a speaking gig, a concert—rather than unseen things that might matter more. That tendency to prioritize tasks that affect our image and reputation, that might make people think good or bad of us, over things that actually grow us as people, give us peace or develop us as better human beings. This tyrant is what drives someone to get so tied up in running their mammoth church or nonprofit that they neglect to commune with God or their staff, it is what allows someone to get so invested in their speaking or writing career that they neglect to nurture relationship with their spouse or to invest in their children.

This tyrant takes advantage of the fact that the world only sees what we do from stage when the lights are on! The world doesn't see how we treat our husband or wife. They don't watch as we check into our cellphone while our eight-year-old tries to get our attention.

Tyranny of the outward comes down to what choice we will make and what criteria we will use for making that choice. If we will assign immediate value to our exterior world or if we will attach the most significance to our interior world.

It's if we will choose to work our way around the kitchen cleaning the nitty-gritty out of the nooks and crevices, while

Jesus sits teaching in our living room.[11]

If we will pour our energy into announcing our good deeds or if we will not let our left hand know what the right one is doing.[12]

It's if we will invest our time praying out in the streets instead of in the closet.[13]

It's if we'll condemn a crying woman who uncomfortably breaks social norms to pour perfume out at our feet. Or if we'll honor her for the motive in her heart regardless of public opinion.[14]

If we will prioritize cleaning the outside of the cup, but leaving the inside of our cups dirty.[15]

If we will whitewash our tomb to camouflage the fact that it houses unclean and dead things inside.[16]

Life can too easily get away from us when we unintentionally just follow whatever daily rhythm we fall into. When we do not take a moment to reflect on what values are guiding our decision making. But when it comes to their own habits, the wise will choose awareness.

They will refuse to kneel down to tyrants.

ALWAYS HAVE
ONE LAST TRY IN YOU

HAVE A RALLY CAP
IN YOUR CLOSET

———————— ✕ ————————

*There's nothing as exciting as a comeback—seeing
someone with dreams, watching them fail,
and then getting a second chance.*
—RACHEL GRIFFITHS #worldchangerbook

At some point in my early twenties, my boss came to visit me in my office. This didn't happen often, in fact it may have been the first time it ever did, and so I instantly knew things were out of sorts.

"I think we're going to have to eliminate your area." He spoke with overt sadness. "We are taking on too many priorities that require too much energy and we can't afford the time and resources it will take."

This, I immediately realized, was the tactful way of alerting me that a pink slip was coming.

But that is a hard thing to unpack to an idealistic young twentysomething who is smack-dab in the middle of her most recent plot to change the world.

I took a deep breath, settled my rattled nerves, looked him straight in the eyes, and said, "No."

I continued, "If you want to tell me that you're downsizing my area because you don't believe in it, because it isn't a value here, because it doesn't fit within our mission, then go ahead. I will walk out the door with respect. But I will not accept you eliminating my area because it's hard . . . because it's hard to find resources or to invest energy in it. It being too hard is not a good reason."

It was a crazy move, maybe even what some people would call reckless, and I had no idea what impact it would have. Would it hurt my relationship with my employer or my credibility within the organization? Would it create lasting tension?

But when someone tells you you're near extinction, you have literally nothing to lose. So you might as well rally.

I kept my job that day. And if it taught me one thing, it was the importance of a rally. Of digging deep, calling on everything you have—every scrap of boldness and humility in the face of vulnerability—and declaring a comeback.

A professor once told a related story. When he was applying to various colleges, he sent out his résumé, which included his research and writings related to *War and Peace.* Only whoops, what did he discover *after* the mail went out?

Instead of saying *War and Peace,* his résumés read *War and Peach.*

Knowing that it would reflect poorly on him, the professor's mind raced to think what he might do to remedy the mistake. Send another résumé with the typo corrected and beg them to swap it out? Hope they wouldn't toss both in the trash? No, desperate circumstances called for desperate measures, so he came up with a funnier rally cry than that.

He found a photo of a painting that had been created to capture the essence of *War and Peace.* And then he found the image of a peach. He cut out the peach, pasted it on the painting, and photocopied it. And he sent it to the employers with a note, saying, *You may have thought War and Peach was a typo, but perhaps it is only because you are unaware of the equally striking classic, War and Peach.*

It was funny! Perhaps a little foolish to some. But it got the rally message across: *Even if it makes me a little vulnerable and silly looking, it is more important to me that you know—without a doubt—that I want to do this. That I believe I can.*

Or let's think for a minute about the athletic arena. Have you ever seen the fans at a baseball stadium rally? They look absolutely ridiculous.

As their team falters and the opponents run up the score and it looks like all is lost, the crazed supporters in the bleachers begin to call for a rally by turning their baseball hats inside out and putting them back on their heads.

How silly, we cry.

Maybe.

But how beautiful too.

How beautiful that in life, when someone or something is about to go under, that a person might be willing to make themselves look silly or vulnerable to express their belief that it's not over yet. To speak vision over the world, over themselves, and over whoever they are supporting, that the best days may still yet be to come.

I promise you, if you champion your goals long enough, life will provide you with many days when it looks like things are going under. I think then a rally cap might be a good investment. I suggest you get one as soon as possible.

RISK & CONTROL

Give me a lever long enough and a fulcrum

on which to place it, and I shall move the world.

—ARCHIMEDES #worldchangerbook

INVALIDATING CRITICS ENTHRONED ON THE SIDELINES

THE MAN IN THE ARENA

———✖———

If my critics saw me walking over the Thames,
they would say it was because I couldn't swim.

—MARGARET THATCHER #worldchangerbook

Isn't it a tragedy when we let fear of criticism prevent us from taking a risk? When we let naysayers sideline us for doing good?

I think it's time to call our critics what they often are.

Not authorities, but cowards.

I'm not talking about dear friends, about those who love you and support you, who sometimes offer push back to what you're doing in life. If they are in it with you, they are not among your critics, they are allies.

I'm talking about the people on the sidelines. The people who won't remember to wish you a happy birthday, who will never buy your kid a graduation gift, who don't bring you soup or cheer when you are sick. I'm talking about the jokers who barely know you well enough to recognize you in an elevator. The people who know you only as much as a friend of a friend of a Facebook friend.

We must take back the silly power we assign to the words of our observers. What a sad ending it would be for each of us and our dreams to have our epithet read not that we were beat down or defeated by forces of evil, or not to have been crushed by our opponents. But to say we were relegated to the sidelines by cowards, taken out of the game by people who aren't even participating in it.

How does this even make sense?

When we are looking for an opinion on a literary classic, do we contact someone we know hasn't read anything since their middle-school comic books? When we want to know about Indy car racing, do we call up our grandma who is nervous to drive down the street at 5 mph for fear of swiping a mailbox? When we want to know about domesticating pit bulls, do we call up someone who has never even owned a goldfish?

Why would we ever assign authority to someone *on the sidelines*?

I choose instead to return to the words of Teddy Roosevelt, as he gave a speech titled "Citizenship in a Republic" in Paris, France:

> It is not the critic who counts; not the man who points out how the strong man stumbles, or where the doer of deeds could have done them better. The credit belongs to the man who is actually in the arena, whose face is marred by dust and sweat and blood; who strives valiantly; who errs, who comes short again and again, because there is no effort without error and shortcoming; but who does actually strive to do the deeds; who knows great enthusiasms, the great devotions; who spends himself in a worthy cause; who at the best knows in the end the triumph

of high achievement, and who at the worst, if he fails, at least fails while daring greatly, so that his place shall never be with those cold and timid souls who neither know victory nor defeat.[1]

Does your heart not echo these words? Does something inside of you not want to stand up and say, *Yes! That is right! I would not want to be the one who never feels deeply, who sits passively on the sideline, who will never be able to describe to someone else what victory tastes like. Not in a million years! A thousand times out of a thousand, I would rather be the one who has endured both highs and lows and has indulged both the sweetness of triumph and the bitterness of defeat, but who at least can describe what it feels like to be truly alive!*

It's time we call those critics' bluff.

How can they take a speck out of our eye when they have a log in theirs?[2] And how can they even see our speck as they sit sidelined on the log as we charge by?

It's time we relegate the feedback of critics to the appropriate filing box—the ones archived into "storage" by the trash collectors every Wednesday. And the awesome thing is, it doesn't matter whether your unknown critic is an obscure blogger or a top-notch reporter from the nation's most prominent newspaper. The words of the smallest or most elite critics can be rolled up and thrown away just the same.

DOING THE RIGHT THING IS BETTER THAN DOING THE SAFE THING

THE LIFE OF IRENA SENDLER

Avoiding danger is no safer in the long run than outright exposure. The fearful are caught as often as the bold.

—HELEN KELLER #worldchangerbook

Do you know Irena Sendler? If you do, you may already understand this principle. If you don't, you must read on.

Irena was a social worker living in Warsaw when Germany began to occupy Poland in 1939. The next year, the Germans got even more blatant and they sanctioned off a ghetto—a walled part of the city where they forced Jews to live apart from the rest of the population.

Things went from bad to worse.

When the Germans' intentions became deadly, Irena could have safely practiced routine social work, written papers, run off the track.

But instead, she chose a more dangerous path.

Irena determined to get into the ghetto. Some reports say she applied to be a sewer or plumbing specialist. And she got clearance to work in this field inside the ghetto. Others claim she obtained fake identification as a nurse and gained permission to practice medicine inside the walled area. Perhaps it was both. What was clear is she didn't run for the hills trying to save her own hide but did the opposite. She went in.

Somewhere in the course of going in and trying to help, she formed a plan. Not just for herself but for ten female friends, a group that eventually grew to twenty-five women, to help her rescue Jewish children before they were sent to concentration camps or otherwise exterminated.

Together, the twenty-five women smuggled children out of the ghetto. They were massively creative. They scrunched the children into suitcases and boxes. They sedated the babies and carried them out in coffins. They used basements, manholes, sewer passages. Any way to get them behind the scenes, underground, off the radar.

The children were taken to Polish families, many of whom were Catholics, and given false names. But Irene carefully recorded their birth identities onto papers that she rolled up and placed in bottles that she buried in her friend's garden. After enduring imprisonment and torture, and later freed through a bribe handed over by friends on the outside, Sendler eventually dug up the bottles and tried to reunite children with their families . . . the few who still had any family living.

Irena took risks beyond what most of us will face in our lifetimes. But do we really think, for a second, that she ever thought of the 2,500 children she and her friends are credited with saving and thought . . . *I wish I hadn't risked it. I wish I hadn't put myself in danger or taken on extra burdens?*

Of course not! How could she feel good about succeeding according to societal norms if she compromised her own conscience?

Do we suspect her deathbed was filled with regrets? *I'd be a lot more satisfied with my life if I had just protected my income and my retirement, if I'd stuck to paying off my mortgage.*

Absolutely not! What would she profit if she won the whole world and lost her own soul?[3]

Irena Sendler knew something deeply, not just something written on paper but something branded onto the pages of her life. A sacrifice-lined life lived in passion is better than an indulgent, pain-free life lived without it.

ONLY TAKE RESPONSIBILITY FOR YOURSELF

YOU DON'T HAVE TO LIVE OUT EVERY PERSON'S BAD DAYS

I cannot trust a man to control others who cannot control himself.

—ROBERT E. LEE #worldchangerbook

I can tell you in a single sentence something that will lend to your contentment at home, at church, in your workplace, or with your cause:

Insist on taking responsibility for yourself and insist on not taking responsibility for others.

So perhaps you are a wife or a husband, a boyfriend or a girlfriend. And perhaps your life is hooked to a partner or even a friend who experiences a wide range of emotion. Who is even a little bit, dare I say it, moody.

At first you may take each of this person's bad moods on with genuine seriousness. You might talk to them about it, you might make them dinner, you might encourage them to rest. You might feel so sincerely plagued by their state of being that you carry their unhappiness around with you all day.

You might stay up late thinking about it, lose sleep and appetite over it, even cry tears over it!

But the older you get, the more you realize that choosing

to do this is insane. Yes, encourage them. Send them cards. Make their favorite dessert. Wish them well! Laugh when they laugh, mourn when they mourn, and help them bear their burdens.

But for goodness' sake, don't replace your own identity or emotional state with theirs. What good does it do the world if you ship out your steadiness, your good feeling, your sanity in exchange for someone else's rockiness, their bad feeling, their ill state of mind? Is the planet better off after you've added yet another unhappy person to it?

And how unfair and disproportionate is this! Is this really what God wants? That you must not only deal with your own bad days but that you must also take on someone else's? So you must have twice as many bad days as the next guy? If this is the case, I hope you don't make too many close friends or your family doesn't ever grow too large. You could get so busy living other people's bad days that you would never have any unoccupied days left to be good!

Really? Is this what God wants? Instead of just mom being burdened by frustration or overcome with grief, now it is mom and dad struggling under the weight of it? Two parents out of commission? Is this what is best for your children?

Don't mishear me. I am not saying don't help others bear their burdens. I'm saying don't give up your right to manage their burdens differently than they choose to! No rule says that when you bear their burdens you can't be smarter or wiser about how you hold them. No rule says you have to mourn as they do, that you must let their grief consume your life. Bearing someone else's burden does not mean handling your emotions just like they do. It does not cancel out your charge to employ what you know.

You are not responsible for how they manage your emotions, but you are still responsible for how you manage yours.

You have been called to rejoice—to set your mind on whatever is noble.[4] To trust that God will work out with them what is between him and them and that the one mediator needed in this scenario is not you.[5]

LET OTHERS PLAY THEIR ROLE TOO

PEOPLE DON'T BELONG TO YOU

———————— ✖ ————————

We believe that what we possess we don't ultimately own. God is merely entrusting it to us.

—JONATHAN SACKS #worldchangerbook

Are you dating? Married? Do you have a family member or an especially close friend? A mentor? Someone who is such a rich part of your life that it makes you prize . . . *and also protect* . . . the unique bond between you?

Tricky, tricky.

Does it ever give rise to sticky, awkward . . . even jealous, competitive . . . thoughts? Do you struggle to share them with others? Do you want to believe that you are the only human being on the planet capable of connecting with them on a meaningful level? Do you find yourself resenting the people they serve?

I once chatted with Lori Wilhite, who runs a site focused on the health and well-being of pastors' families. She told me she was at a conference for Christian leaders when the person onstage called out the family members of church leaders who were in attendance.

Of course the pastor's greatest responsibility is to his family, he noted. But then he posed a potentially life- and behavior-altering question: *Can you imagine how you would feel if your desperate grip on your spouse's life prevented them from fully doing all that God is stirring them to do?*

If your jealousy made the work of the kingdom smaller? If it short-circuited their potential to influence others' spiritual well-being? If it brought about bad for those who served them?

This is what led the apostle Paul to say what he said, right? To say, I would prefer men who serve to be unmarried so they can be laser-focused on pleasing the Lord. But once you add marriage and family to the equation, they may feel divided between pleasing God and pleasing a spouse![6]

Do you know what that means then, friends? You—the loved, the family, the endeared companions—are often the most important permission giver in their lives. The people who can best free up their mental and emotional space, who can perhaps most powerfully create grace for their busy stretches and most completely dissolve their anxieties, those who can most bless their investment of time in the larger community, in the mission of Christ, in the greater good.

You can give them a gift no one else can.

The gift of freeing them from the bondage of living purely for your benefit and the gift of freeing them to live toward what God wants for them.

This is the only logical thing to do, don't you think?

Along these lines, I once spoke to a retired couple who recounted how, in their earlier years, they'd had a scare with one of their children.

Their very young child had been hit by a car. As the parents followed the ambulance to the hospital, something terrifying happened.

Without warning, it pulled off to the side of the road and came to a stop.

And the worst thoughts, the natural thoughts that would jump into any parents' heads, crept into theirs.

Their child was on the brink of death, they suspected. *Perhaps had even died.*

As their hearts raced and ached and they sat in the unknowing, they prayed. And the words they recounted they prayed have never left me.

God, we fear the worst for our child, but we know he never belonged to us, but to you. Thank you for allowing us the years you have given us so far.

Their child lived and grew up to be healthy and unscathed by the accident in the long run, but to me, the climax of the story was not the child's outcome but the uncanny prayer they spoke in the midst of possible disaster.

A prayer of openhandedness, which does not assume to God the right to clutch at other people, to determine the outcome of their lives, to act as though they are deeded—as human beings—to us as possessions.

A prayer that throws off the impulses of slavery, not just in commercial transactions but in fully believing even those dearest to us were born children who belong first and foremost to their Creator.

We welcome others into our lives. We attach to them. We shepherd them. We enjoy knowing and being known.

But we rejoice that we have not been given as luxury items, pseudorobots to be programmed and controlled. But that we stand next to them—our spouses, our children, our friends, our loved ones—in belonging together to God.

ALIGNMENT & RELATIONSHIPS

You realize you can't change the world
but it shouldn't stop you from trying.
—KEVIN JOHNSON #worldchangerbook

DON'T GO TO THE FINISH LINE ALONE

THE BEAUTY OF RECOGNIZING YOUR ALSO-DEDICATED FRIENDS

Alone we can do so little; together we can do so much.
—HELEN KELLER #worldchangerbook

I trust you're determined to stick it out. To run the course. To finish well.

Good for you!

Here is my request:

Please do not go to the finish line alone. Take someone with you.

Sound strange? Maybe. Just because this is not the mantra being chanted in our culture, is it? We're taught something different. How to break away from the pack, to set ourselves apart.

We—those of us in the ministry world, mission field, humanitarian arena—are taught survival of the fittest. There is an implied bottom line: some will stand strong, some will get squashed, and still others will stand on their squashed heads and be platformed.

There are only so many megachurches in the fields of hometown faith. There are only so many speakers staged at the few prominent conferences . . . only so many book deals granted by the limited number of publishers . . . recording contracts put out by a finite group of music labels . . . donation dollars awarded by a fixed number of philanthropists . . . feature articles printed and posted in a set number of popular magazines and websites. So get in now, get yours, snatch everything up you can, before the marketplace gets saturated, right?

Because, as much as we hate it, we cannot all win. Every cause cannot prevail. If everyone won, then no one would! Right?

Please tell me you sense deep down that conclusion is wrong.

Who could ever get to the finish line, look back at their fallen comrades littering the battlefield, and feel good? Would that be cause for celebration? To be near the end and know that you, and you alone, made it! You've become the *most* successful. You're head and shoulders above the rest!

Congratulations. Let us heap medals on you until you cannot move. Here's a beautiful library where you can grow old and die while reading your own bestsellers. Is that living the dream?

If you are trying to do good in this world at the expense of other people who are doing good, then I have news for you: you are no longer on the side of good.

Those who do good want the most good for all people.

If someone else does good, then good is accomplished.

The more of us there are, the more faith and justice take hold.

We who invest our lives in cause, in faith, we cannot afford the luxury of selfishness. We must take seriously

Paul's insistence we do nothing from rivalry or conceit, but in humility count others more significant than ourselves. To not only watch out for our own interests, but also for the interests of others.[1]

Please. Don't do the world the disservice of going alone.

SOMETIMES GOOD INVOLVES RISK; DO GOOD ANYWAY

YOU BE THE SOMEONE ELSE

———————⬛———————

He who sees a need and waits to be
asked for help is as unkind as if he had refused it.

—DANTE ALIGHIERI #worldchangerbook

Social norms are a funny thing.

They're what enable us to get along. To function amidst other people. To be tolerable.

Understanding them saves us from being that loud or close talker. From tweeting and posting Facebook updates about all the intricate, personal details of our emotional state. It's what allows us to recognize when a conversation has run its course, when it's time to excuse oneself. To stop talking and go home.

Socialization squashes bad behavior, excessive vulnerability, reckless transparency.

But it can also sadly choke out some of the good stuff too.

You walk into a restaurant and see an older person sitting alone, eating. It strikes you that while they certainly may just prefer peace and quiet, that they also may have aged into a lonelier station in life. One where a spouse or many friends have passed away.

Maybe your compassionate leanings start to prick at your

heart then. Your sensibilities suggest you should invite them to sit with you. Or to attempt to join them at their table. At the least, to welcome conversation . . . belonging, at some small level.

But then comes the voice of your conditioning.

Please! That could be awkward. What if she's just waiting for her granddaughter? What if he's a hermit who comes here to check out of small talk in some small corner with his newspaper? What if I make her feel uncomfortable, obligated? Keeping him company is someone else's role.

Or you're speaking to some acquaintance. Someone you've come upon several times, with whom you've come to engage in small talk. And in the course of conversation or life events, you come into information that is a little bit beyond the scope of your normal chitchat about the weather or local sports. You find out he was just divorced or went bankrupt, she just got a DUI or was a victim of domestic abuse.

Your emotions piece together an internal auto-response that meets the person where they are. *This should never have happened to you. I'm sorry you experienced this. This isn't what God intended,* your soul cries out.

You want to validate. Give the gift of recognition.

To offer connection. A bit of peace. Some blessing.

But perhaps this is too intimate a thing to say. Perhaps it's not my place. This is a conversation for someone else who knows her better than I do.

"So I heard we may get rain again today," your mouth says.

Or you're talking to someone who is much more experienced than you. Someone you look up to, whose accomplishments outweigh your own. And there you are talking to them, being moved by who they are and what they're becoming.

And you want to say, *I'm proud of you. The work you have done? It's been worth it. I know it hasn't been easy. That you've paid the cost. But I'm thankful you hung in there.*

But who are you to say that? Some cut-rate kid? Someone who doesn't know the first thing about their field? Who can't hold a candle to their expertise? Who feels a little awkward or reverent in their presence?

That's for someone else to say.

So you slink away with a, "It was great to meet you. I've read your book."

Or take conversations like this one, for instance.

My grandmother, a well-meaning and protective motherly type, once suggested it would be unwise for my husband and me to allow a teenager, who'd been convicted of a felony, to move into our house for a couple years.

She was generous. Don't fault her there. But, like any grandma, she sensed possible danger for those she loved.

It's not that she didn't empathize with his need or want him to be helped. She just was hoping the help wouldn't come from us. Her exact words? *Let someone else do that.*

Let someone else do that?

But how could this well-meaning suggestion be right? Particularly for those who claim the faith, who have the nerve to profess John 15:13's description of the greatest love? Of idealizing a life laid down for a friend?

How could we simultaneously claim a love that holds up physically laying a life down if we are not even willing to lay down our conveniences, preferences, or ease in living detached from other people's problems?

Despite her warnings, my husband and I opted to invite this teenager to live with us.

Rather than ask him, the vulnerable in need of support, to understand why we couldn't open our lives to him, we asked her, in her comfort and sufficiency, to understand why we could.

It was one of the best choices I've ever made.

I don't have a whole dissertation to explain why that move made sense for us. I only have this simple conviction:

Too many times, I don't think there is someone else.

I think you and I might be the only someone else there is.

RELATIONSHIPS AS A LINE OF CREDIT

INVEST ENOUGH AND YOU MAY SCORE SOME FREE APPLE PIE

We make a living by what we get,
but make a life by what we give.

—WINSTON CHURCHILL #worldchangerbook

The strangest thing happened at one of those twenty-four-hour restaurants one day.

It sounds like a setup for a joke, but it's true.

I was in high school and I was working there as a waitress, saving for college.

I was waiting on a table of two diners, a man and his teenage son, who seemed to be doing fine, just like any other table. Suddenly, almost abruptly however, the dad flagged me down.

"I need to speak with the manager right away," he said urgently.

I nodded and assured him I'd retrieve my supervisor, of course reviewing the diner's experience in my head, fearing complaints.

But instead, as my manager approached the table, the man broke into confession. "I just realized I don't have enough money on me to pay the full bill. I'm so sorry. Could my son maybe come back with you and wash a few dishes or do some work to cover where we fall short?"

Since I have a little bit of a bleeding heart at times, I was immediately horrified on the man's behalf. I quickly and quietly tried to signal my manager that I'd be willing to cover the shortage myself to save this man any prolonged awkwardness.

"Nah!" My manager waved me off and then in a twist that surprised me, she added, "It's on the house. You guys have a great day."

Since this was not a family-owned restaurant but a chain bogged down with all kinds of corporate policies, I was shocked by her generosity. I expressed my surprise and she responded with a clarifying statement that stuck with me.

"*Today* it's on the house. Gladly. Now if he comes up short again tomorrow," she said with a grin, "that's a different story."

Huh, I thought. That one simple line transfers to so many contexts.

You ask for help from someone today? Fine.

You ask them to endure a long conversation about something that is important to you? Maybe.

You ask them to be patient with you while you give them negative feedback? Okay.

One withdrawal here and there? No big deal. We can skim it off the top and it doesn't affect our health or profitability.

But if we become known as the needy, always asking for one more thing, who always wants to distract us in a long winding conversation, who always wants to vent their negative commentary, who always wants to offer unsolicited advice?

When it's all withdrawals and no deposits?

Well that starts to impact a person's bottom line.

This wasn't the only time the restaurant business drove this point home.

There was also Mrs. Smith, an older lady who came in every single day and sat in the first booth on the left in our restaurant. And if her booth was occupied, there was no directing her to another table.

"I'll wait," Mrs. Smith insisted. And then she would hand us a stack of the plastic to-go containers we periodically gave her, which she had taken home and washed. "So you can reuse them. I put 'em in the dishwasher; they're good as new!"

It was no use explaining health code at that point, we found. It was easier to just thank her and file them in the trash can in the back of the restaurant.

I still remember the first time I waited on Mrs. Smith. The first time she ordered her "usual" with me—the senior spaghetti dinner.

When she'd finished her meal, Mrs. Smith looked up at me expectantly and said, "I'll take my free slice of apple pie now."

"Your free slice of pie?" I repeated.

"Yes, the one on special."

Knowing enough not to argue with the customer, I returned to the same manager, confused.

"There's a lady at table 13 who says we have free apple pie on special," I reported.

"Oh, that's Mrs. Smith," the manager replied, without even looking up from her paperwork. "She's been coming in every day for years. She still thinks we're running this free dessert special we offered three years ago. We just play along."

Ha! I thought, delighted at the corporation's generosity. "I never knew a corporation had a heart!"

"Well, we do." She added, "And the bottom line is we also have a brain. Mrs. Smith comes in and buys a dinner and a drink every single night. A couple times a week she brings a friend, or a table full of family with her. The profit she brings us more than pays for those free slices of apple pie."

And there I had it.

If you're new on the scene, your entitlement is low. You don't get to expect any special favors. But as long as you keep making deposits, as long as you're contributing, you're making investments in the system, you may just score some free apple pie from time to time.

Lesson noted.

THE FIRST FOLLOWER

DANCING ON A HILLSIDE

———————✕———————

*The first follower publicly
shows everyone else how to follow.*
—DEREK SIVERS #worldchangerbook

I could've included several Derek Sivers quotes because he has something worth hearing. And the video he presented during his TED Talk (which you can see at sarahcunningham. org/the-first-follower) highlights an insight that is easily observable as we watch everyday leadership play out around us.

The video content is short and simple, but its premise would stick with me for life even if I'd only seen it one time. It's that good.

(Seriously. Take a second and go watch it.)

And referencing it leads me back to a slightly subversive question: Who says the leader is the most important person in the movement?

Is the most significant contributor always the one onstage?

Is the person most responsible for an idea's success always the one listed as the founder, executive director, or CEO?

(Anyone who has met a good executive assistant at a large company, nonprofit, school, or megachurch might easily argue otherwise.)

And—hold on to your armrests—could the opposite even be true?

Could it be, even, that at least some of the time, taking seat number two might accomplish even more than seat number one?

That recognizing and supporting a good idea might sometimes be even more important than being the one to launch it?

That there might be just as much to learn from being a follower as there is from being a leader?

Not sure? Well, are you game to find out?

If so, here's my challenge: find something this year that you can be the follower in.

That's where it starts (but not, as you may have guessed, where it ends).

Then determine to not just be *a* follower but to be the most supportive follower this person has ever experienced.

Sounds weird, right? That's because in our culture, we're way more used to hearing people aspire to lead things to their fullest, not to be the champion follower.

That's okay though. Forget what you know about that.

And think broadly.

This challenge doesn't have to be a formal operation. It doesn't have to be going down to the local Salvation Army and pledging to ring bells for a set number of hours next Christmas season or signing up for the three-month rotation at the nearest church nursery.

It can be way more organic than that. Pick out some person—any age, gender, location, field—who you are convinced is doing good in this world. Now make some sort of internal self-pledge that goes like this: I now resolve that it is part of my vocation to make sure this person feels supported.

And go with whatever serves that end.

Maybe it's being one of those rare people who get over awkwardness and tells them straight up that you believe in them. Maybe it's sending a thank-you note for what they've contributed to you, others, the world. Maybe it's just letting them know someone noticed all their efforts. Maybe it's showing interest, not just passing curiosity but truly, vested interest, in what is happening in their lives or organization. Maybe it's offering to extend yourself for them. To watch their kids or to house-sit, to connect them with your agent or your car mechanic, to help them develop an idea, to share about them, to spread their links around your social networks. Maybe it's resourcing them: sending a good book, forwarding an article, passing on some information.

You start figuring out, choppily at first, what kinds of things might be helpful. What's not enough. What's irrelevant. What's too much.

And then suddenly, you've learned something that is transferable. And if it's something great like affirming other people and their work, it mounts inside you. It feeds positive momentum. It makes you want to try it again. To extend yourself to someone else.

Then before you know it, a few intentional acts get inside you. The value of those acts prove themselves right and real to you. They seep their way into your identity and into the fabric of your personality. And before you realize it, extending yourself in support of people becomes less of a calculated choice and more of a habit. It becomes the outflowing of who you are.

I am not naturally encouraging. I have a sarcastic bent. I can be cynical, snarky, overzealous. But on my good days, this sort of intentionality is no longer calculated. It's taken up residence in me.

I'm slowly, with much stumbling and wrong turns, becoming a better follower every day. And it has only added good to my life.

LOOK FOR
THE COMMON THREAD

A LIST OF THINGS
ALL HUMANS HAVE IN COMMON

——————————————

*People are pretty much alike.
It's only that our differences are more
susceptible to definition than our similarities.*

—LINDA ELLERBEE #worldchangerbook

Go back to childhood. To those fragile, gangly, awkward days when you were just figuring out who you were.

How did your ideas about your own identity come together?

It was probably a mixture of things, right?

The way you were treated or the values and beliefs you were taught by your parents or whoever raised you. The worldviews and ideas of your extended family or friends or parents of your friends. The norms in your community or school. The books you read, the movies you watched, or the music you listened to.

Through some series of information and events and thoughts, consciously or subconsciously, you began to collect ideas and absorb them.

Yes, this is what I think. This reflects who I am. This is how I was raised to be. This is me.

Perhaps less obviously, your identity was also influenced

by another set of ideas. These ideas were things your parents or mentors or peers *didn't* believe in. The things they spoke out against. The things they didn't like or avoided or made you avoid.

It was the unkindness of a bully. The laziness of a neighbor. The reckless choices of an addict. Certain words and behaviors.

That is not what I think. That is not who I am. That is not who I was raised to be. This is not me.

All of this is important. It's well and good. We can't enter into adolescence or adulthood, can't find our passion, choose our vocation, ascribe to mission, prioritize our time, or invest in a cause without defining who we are in this world.

But if you've ever learned about Jungian theory, you know it suggests that by default, usually not consciously, we start defining ourselves using these weird black-and-white, either/or kinds of categories.

That is me. That is not me. They are like me. They are not like me.

And herein, of course, is the problem.

Life and people do not fit so neatly into either/or sorts of categories.

That selfish person over there?

We don't necessarily see them through the same gracious filter we use to view ourselves.

We tend to snap judge the surface.

That is not who I am. That is not how I think or behave. That is not what I like. You are not like me.

But oh, oh, oh—wait, before you lodge that too deep in your soul—be sure. Are they really not like you?

Or is it at all possible, as my friend Mike Foster's book *Gracenomics* suggests, that you caught them at a bad moment? That on an off day, in a tired stretch, you glimpsed a very unusual showing of their self-absorption?

What if, in fact, you *both* value unselfishness, but you both occasionally break your norm and display something less than your own intentions?

When really if we stopped looking only for the things that we are not like, focusing so quickly on the things that divide us, maybe we could reframe things and start with acknowledging the similarities we share in all being humans, made in God's image, loved and pursued by him, on this plot of ground we call our home.

Even baseline, bottom-row things that make up much of our shared existence. Like almost all, if not all, human beings:

Are born
Need food, water, and shelter from the elements
Have similar body parts, senses, and biological functions
Grow and change as time passes
Are raised in families (often, to a smaller or greater
     extent, imperfect families)
Are reared in the context of a larger community of
     some sort
Have free will
Make a friend
Own or strive to own something they value
Learn
Have expectations put on them
Get sick

Experience love for someone

Feel pain at another's hand

Smile, frown, laugh, cry

Suffer

Have a secret

Have lied

Have experienced guilt

Have argued or fought (or wanted to) over something

Marry or attend a wedding

See a medical professional for an injury or disease or
   are impacted by someone who does

Desire to survive

Experience fear

Use language, which is sometimes fallible and
   sometimes fails us, to communicate

Are at risk of natural disasters or impacted by weather

Have potential to do both good and evil

Desire to be successful or productive

Desire to belong

Desire to be significant

Search for meaning

Adopt values

Try to discern truth

Desire to find contentment

Are frustrated by things that are outside their control

Live with knowledge their bodies are deteriorating

Live understanding they will one day die

Have the same Creator

Have the same ability to sin

Have the same grace given to us

Have the same Savior born to us
Have the same salvation available to us
Have the same ability to pray and be heard by God

There is so much of human experience that connects us to each other, that allows us to meaningfully engage others in the very matters that matter most—matters of existence, of meaningful living, of contentment and suffering, sickness and health, life and of death.

What more would we offer the world if we were able to stop dis-identifying? To remind ourselves that although we are different, and sometimes different in important theological, intellectual, and behavioral ways, that in our difference we have much likeness.

THE SAD IRONY OF BREAKING RANKS

THE PRESS RELEASES JESUS DIDN'T SEND OUT

———————— ✖ ————————

We have enough religion to make us hate,
but not enough to make us love one another.

—JONATHAN SWIFT #worldchangerbook

Something that haunts me is breaking ranks.

To delineate in a way that won't satisfy all of you, I'll note I'm all for difference of opinion, for holding to your convictions, standing your ground. All day long.

But sometimes, honestly asserting what we believe seems to cross this hazy line into a kind of sticky image management, where we make it our policy to take the stage (or send out a press release or post an open letter to whomever) for the express purpose of dividing ourselves from others.

At a recent public event attended by people of diverse traditions, a pastor prayed publicly. The occasion was to remember victims of a tragic occurrence. But this pastor was reprimanded by a leader from his denomination for participating with those who had differences on various points of faith from his—and he later apologized, even recanting his prayer.

Really?

Naturally the incident went viral and the denominational leader eventually backed off.

I understand the sectarian dynamics at play, but it's troubling that a group of believers could tell the world it was more important, in the name of Christ, to disassociate from that prayer that day than it was to let that act of kindness, offered in the name of Jesus, stand.

I won't, however, disassociate myself from the pastor who offered the apology or even from the one who demanded it. I know what it's like to feel torn between doing what you think is right and doing what some particular religious camp might expect of you. As the pastor found, there's a tension in wanting to bear witness to Christ while at the same time not giving the impression that legitimate differences of doctrine don't matter.

So I have to claim my identity next to those who habitually but probably unintentionally sometimes skew God's grace in tasteless ways.

But I still can't help pointing out the terrible irony at work when this happens. How I'm pretty sure if Jesus was walking the planet in this era, a lot of contemporary Christians would demand he issue a press release to clarify he was just *eating with the drunks, but he himself is not a drunk.* That we'd pressure him to post something on his blog to stress *the prostitute just tags along after him, but he doesn't embrace her as a member of his team.* That we'd ask him to issue a public apology for *teaching in the synagogue, lest he accidentally give people the impression he—like some of those in the room who believed differently—didn't accept the Messiah.*

A TIP FOR PERSEVERING IN ANY RELATIONSHIP

HAPPINESS VS. HOLINESS

———————◄►———————

Every adversity, every failure, every heartache carries with it the seed of an equal or greater benefit.

—NAPOLEON HILL #worldchangerbook

Here's one simple insight from an author that I immediately applied and that improved almost every relationship I had.

The book was geared to husbands and wives, especially to those moments when spouses grow tired of each other. It was aimed at that moment when a husband looks at his partner, sick and disheveled and crying her eyes out, and thinks, *I can't believe I married this person.* Or directed at the moment when a wife, exhausted by her husband's recent failure to contribute, buries her face in her hands and declares, *This marriage is doomed. He does not make me happy!*

And the one idea I took from this author applies not only to this situation and to marriage but to every sort of companionship or commitment we hold.

It pokes at the attitudes that arise in our hearts on our worst days, when that spouse, parent, child, relative, coworker, friend, or neighbor fails to meet our self-identified needs and we, in turn, are disappointed.

Frazzled.

Skeptical.

Wondering if it is time to end this relationship that does not, in fact, make us happy.

And here is the concept, both simple and profound but with far-reaching implications, which I took from Gary Thomas[2] that day and carried into each day forward.

What if God did not bring this person into your life solely to make you happy? What if God also put them there to make you holy?

Section 6
PLANS & PRIORITIES

It is more rewarding to watch money
change the world than watch it accumulate.

—GLORIA STEINEM #worldchangerbook

WE DON'T HAVE TO FIND GOD'S WILL FOR OUR LIVES

GOD'S WILL IS KNOWN

All we have to decide is what to do with the time that is given to us.

—GANDALF THE GREY #worldchangerbook

We have to find God's will for our lives.

We just have to!

. . . Or do we?

No, I'm not dismissing the importance of seeking to understand God and live out his principles. No question, God designed life to include certain outcomes. To be productive, for instance, to build families,[1] to experience life to the full.[2] Those are all givens in my book. Probably in yours too.

What I'm really asking is, what does will finding look like? What *should* it look like? And where did we get our ideas about this whole process?

When some people talk about God's will, I don't always buy all they're selling. For example, are God's intentions really so camouflaged that we must pick apart the planet to find them? That we have to carefully examine the events of every day and every setting, hoping to be attentive enough to correctly piece together some underground plan he has drafted for our lives? That if we accidentally pass over a clue he's planted, we'll never find God's will for our lives?

When did the search for God's will become a Nicholas Cage movie?

Or a race for the five golden tickets randomly wrapped among millions of candy bars?

Does the God of the Bible work like that? The being who hung the stars in space to declare his glory?[3] Who lit the heavens with the sun and sprinkled clouds across the horizon so all people would see his glory?[4] Does it sound like the God who wrote his eternal strength and divine nature into everything he made, so that his invisible qualities could be understood by all?[5]

Do these verses portray someone who is in hiding? Who covertly communicates with us through buried messages? It makes me wonder.

Not to mention I can't think of a single person to whom Jesus said, "Get out your magnifying glass. Pay attention to everything you see, every single day. Verily, verily, I say unto you, God has hidden clues that—if put together correctly— will lead you to the particular blueprint for your life."

So am I denying God is mysterious? No. God is a holy enigma, for sure. He has both traits that are knowable and dimension that keeps us growing and yearning to understand more. What he does next often catches us by surprise.

But here's the thing.

Our expedition to discover God's will, in my opinion, probably doesn't have to take us much farther than our own bedrooms or living rooms . . . or wherever the nearest Bible is sitting.

Might there be a few things, specific to us, that God

wants us to pursue? That is altogether possible.

But may I humbly suggest something before you, especially those of you who are young, wait paralyzing years looking for signs, waiting for God to pick up a Sharpie and write something on your bedroom wall or waiting for the sunset to audibly scream your name?

A whole lot about God's will is *not* a mystery.

In the creation narrative, God told Adam and Eve to be fruitful, to multiply, to make good use of the earth. That's pretty direct.

And Jesus said "the will of my Father" is that everyone who looks on the Son will believe and have eternal life.[6]

You don't exactly need a decoder ring to figure out that one either.

Or take the command Jesus himself identified as the greatest. "Love the Lord your God with all your heart and with all your soul and with all your mind." Or, the commandment he assigned to be the second greatest: "Love your neighbor as yourself."[7] Surely something of God's intentions are mixed up in those, right?

Or perhaps most obviously, consider the Great Commission, Jesus' parting instruction to his disciples. Disciple, baptize, teach what I command.[8]

First Thessalonians later adds that giving thanks in all circumstances is the will of God.[9]

And these are just the beginning. We could proof-text hundreds, maybe thousands, of statements that reflect God's direction about human existence.

We grasp that his will was for humans to:

Enter into relationship with him, to declare him our God
    and to identify ourselves as his people, to bring
    blessing to others
Hold him first, honor a Sabbath, to reverence his name
Foster societies that promote the well-being of the whole,
    where we don't steal, kill, or lie
Nurture fair economies, where the needs of the orphaned,
    the widow, the poor are met
Show hospitality to foreigners
Bear the good news, go to all people, turn the other cheek,
    go the extra mile, pray for our enemies
Do not judge, brag, or pray to impress
Gather together, to be kind, to be known by our love

So what about it? Are you doing these things? If so, I have good news for you! You are in God's will.

Are you not doing these things? Then review what you know and go do them and you will be in God's will too!

But what about future things? The possibilities that lie out in front of us?

Is there any chance that based on what we already know, we might be able to get to the bottom of whether some specific action aligns with God's will?

Romans 12, for example, seems to suggest that as we renew our minds and test ideas, we will be able to discern for ourselves.[10]

So what about it? Does doing some new thing shift your priorities away from what you already know of God? Does it make you too busy or too apathetic to observe a Sabbath? Does it make you too consumed with your mission to love the people around you? Does it catch you up in self-admiration, in the love of approval and applause?

Then those things are drifting you away from God's will.

But does the choice in front of you naturally align with the values interlaced through the Scriptures?

Then that is his will! For goodness' sake, get on with it!

Don't be one of those people Jesus must look at and ask, "Why do you call me 'Lord, Lord,' and not do what I say?"[11]

There are better things to do with your life other than to sift through every bag of Lays you can find, searching for some odd potato chip that resembles Jesus.

No matter what, you can always focus on living the part of God's will you already know in whatever situation you find yourself. We know so much of God's will, so entirely much, that even if you never scouted out one specific detail about the occupation in front of you or the destination you're considering, you could still live your entire life just on that. We could busy ourselves for ten lifetimes just living out what we *do* know about God's will.

THERE'S NOT JUST ONE WAY

GOD'S WILL IS NOT A MAZE

———————✖———————

There's not just one possible path.
It's never too late to be what you might have been.

—GEORGE ELIOT #worldchangerbook

While I'm suggesting a great deal of God's will is already known, I don't rule out God may very well have a specific intention for your life, some particular purpose you were born for, expressly gifted for, or being groomed to take on.

I'm not ruling out the possibility that he may even sometimes prompt you toward a specific person to marry or a location to live. By nature of being God, he can do any and all he likes and how he extends himself is not for me to say.

But I think the very idea of God's will being just one thing can be incredibly disserving too. That some of us sometimes lock onto it, become obsessive about it, anxious about it. That we feel intense pressure to find our one path, to get that one thing right. We become convinced if we don't choose the right job opportunity, fall in love with the chosen person, move to the right city, that we might be in deep trouble!

Stop.

For your own sake, stop.

Spiraling thoughts that stir anxiety inside you are likely not helping you get a better hand on God's will. God's will does not look anxious. He has not given us a spirit of fear, but of power and of love and of a sound mind.[12]

And on top of that, please give yourself some breathing room with this idea: God's will is not a maze. It is not a sadistic, supernatural video game. If you take a well-meaning left when God preferred you to go right, he doesn't dead-end your life. He doesn't cut off all possibility for good for you from this time forward.

If you take a job in Georgia instead of Ohio, you don't melt off his radar. He doesn't lose your file folder. His GPS doesn't go down.

What if you marry Angela instead of Erika? Paul instead of Mark? God doesn't refuse to come to Thanksgiving. He doesn't stop inviting you to pool parties at his house. God is not a catty middle-school girl.

That's not how the God of the Bible works. The God of the Bible is so much bigger than that.

He is not some rigid sort of craftsman who is standing above you with a hammer, and can only make something good out of your life if you hold up a nail in the exact right place, at the exact right time.

Even a human carpenter can do better than that. If there are only screws and no nails, they can find a different tool.

Clearly God isn't handcuffed by circumstances more than they are!

God's will can play out through endless series and combinations of circumstances and people. If we truly believe God is all-knowing, it naturally follows that we cannot invent a scenario that sends him back to the drawing board to try to solve. Your worst mistakes can't make the Creator fall off his throne.

As long as you are seeking after him, he sees potential in every place you put your foot. And he can build a masterpiece out of any material that presents itself.

WE PROBABLY AREN'T GOING TO DIE FOR THE FAITH, SO WE SHOULD LEARN TO LIVE FOR IT

WHAT WOULD YOU TAKE A BULLET FOR?

---

*Conviction is worthless
unless it is converted into conduct.*

—THOMAS CARLYLE #worldchangerbook

What are you passionate enough to die for?

Go ahead. Close your eyes. Think about how you would respond. Try to rattle off a list of your most deeply held beliefs. Just like I did when Pedro Windsor Garcia, an urban pastor and community leader, asked me the same question.

All this talk about what I would die for took me back to familiar territory. Back to the pulpits of traveling evangelists, where giving up one's physical life for God was sometimes painted with dramatics.

I conjured up stories about the saints of Rome singing while being martyred in coliseums. I saw images of Cassie Bernall, the girl from Columbine, blinking back tears as someone held a gun to her head and questioned her belief in God.

You know the stories I'm talking about.

Missionaries starving to death after giving away all their food.

People of faith imprisoned in concentration camps or murdered by natives as they tried to champion the gospel.

Underground pastors smuggling the Bible behind enemy lines, under the threat of firing squads.

The common thread stitching together these stories, of course, was ablaze with conviction: *Never deny your faith in Christ. Even at gunpoint or the tip of a sword, your faith is worth dying for.*

Right?

In light of this, my answer to "What are you passionate enough to die for?" is pretty predictable. I would die for . . . my brothers . . . other people I love . . . my faith. I would possibly die to fight extreme injustice. I like to believe I would risk my life for any child under threat of harm. In that kind of life-on-the-line moment, I like to hope I would stand strong for what was important.

You probably do too.

But while I pray we pledge our allegiance with that kind of fierceness, I'd like to suggest that martyrdom heroics aren't always the appropriate approach to our context.

Do martyrs show unexplainably deep courage? Yes!

Do we admire those who literally lay down their lives for their beliefs? Definitely.

But please let me suggest—"What you would die for?"—might not be the best question. It might not be the most pertinent *or likely* question anyway. At least not for those of us living in this era of the postmodern, developed, free world. Maybe our question is the second one Pedro presented:

What are you passionate enough to live *for?*

Go ahead. Think about that one.

What are you passionate enough to live for?

In theory, I've asked you the same question twice. Because *what we say we would be willing to die for should be exactly the same as what we're already living for.*

But what we're actually putting our time into—yard work, laundry, soccer practice, whatever fills up our calendar —doesn't always give away our values on paper, does it?

But it should!

After all, why would anyone believe I would lay down my life—yes, to literally take a bullet—for my younger brothers, for example, if I never figured out how to express commitment or devotion to them in my ordinary life? If I never deferred to their preferences, if I never sacrificed for their well-being, if I celebrated their shortcomings or envied their victories, why would they or anyone else ever believe that I would lay down my life for them?

Similarly, why would God—or better yet, why would the nonreligious—ever see our faith as the most vital, poignant, risk-worthy activity in our lives if we never made the time to internalize and embody it? Why would they think we'd take a bullet if we won't even turn off the TV? To care for the poor if we won't even curb our addiction to shoes or electronic gadgets? To stand up to a militant abuser if we won't take an unpopular stand to defend the oppressed in our workplace or stand up to the everyday bullies in our social spheres? To— under different circumstances—pour out our lives for the poor or the powerless, when we refuse to give up being the power-holders of culture or pulpits?

People know what you would die for by one thing. And one thing alone.

What you live for.

It's a safe bet to say, the way most of us will best impact the world won't likely be through mustering enough courage in any one moment to face a bullet or a sword. But know what I suspect *would* impact the developed, free world far more than this sort of rare, isolated instance of martyrdom? If all those who will never be martyred, who will live out the remainder of their days in relative freedom and comfort, decided they were going to let the beliefs they claim they would die for . . . *inform their living.*

If we stopped with the theatrics about what we'd die for and we did what Paul said. If we presented ourselves a *living* sacrifice.[13]

ALL IDEAS AREN'T EQUALLY VALID

THE TEMPERATURE WHERE WATER FREEZES

———————◆———————

When freedom does not have a purpose . . .
when it does not listen to the voice of conscience,
it turns against humanity and society.

—POPE JOHN PAUL II #worldchangerbook

It's culturally correct to be able to go with the flow. To respect that people have the right to diverse opinions and be able to live in harmony in spite of divergent ideas.

I'd even suggest that when the motives of our heart are rooted in humility, it favors a guy named Jesus. After all, peacemakers are called the children of God.[14]

But while doing everything in your power to keep the peace,[15] we sometimes go beyond just respecting every person's right to think freely to a very different position: we assign any and all ideas equal validity.

This, for me, is sometimes akin to people pleasing. We're so focused on respecting what he or she says that we lose track of what produces good and wholesomeness for ourselves. It's as if we are silently conceding every trail, path, idea leads to the same amount of satisfaction.

But, holy cow. Stop and think about that! Even the most

respectful and accepting among us don't really believe that.

Are you hesitant to say you hold some individuals' ideas to be less valid than others? Are you worried if you admit you don't think their ideas lead to goodness, you will be perceived as intolerant? Closed-minded? Prejudiced? Even bigoted?

Do you think, *I can find something worthwhile in every perspective. Maybe I do think all ideas have merit?*

I know what you're trying to say, but I wonder if you really mean that.

What if someone believes that water doesn't freeze at 32° F? What if she insists water doesn't freeze unless it drops below 0° F? What if she even gets a teaching job and convinces her students it does not freeze unless it drops below 0?

Let's say a snowy, slushy wintery storm falls onto the region all night. In the morning, she gets up and checks the thermometer, sees it is 12° out and is relieved to know that—according to her beliefs—it is still above freezing. If she then pulls out of her driveway, will the road be frozen with ice or will it realign itself to match her belief? If she drives her normal speed to work, believing the roads to be dry, will the car refuse to slip or slide at stop signs? If her students go out into their yards, will the puddles not be iced over on top? Will the icicles fall off their houses?

What if a person believes there are 15 inches in every foot instead of 12? What if he draws up diagrams and writes books and gives dissertations to support his theory? Or blogs about it? When he drives his 14-foot-high truck under an overpass with a 10-foot clearance, will the overpass rise to allow him to pass through based on his beliefs?

Of course not. That's a logical fallacy. It's not conceivable that *all* ideas will bring about the same amount of good.

Don't say you believe nothing!

Fine, say you respect people regardless of what they believe. Say you approach people with humility, that you leave room for the possibility that your own interpretation of how God wants us to live could be mistaken. Yes, by all means, be meek. Good for you. The meek will inherit the earth!

But don't speak so extremely that you validate *everything*.

As my friend Ron once asked, What if I believe it's okay to break into your house and steal your car? Are you okay with that? What if I think it's okay to help myself to your wife or husband? Is that all right by you? What if I'm okay with drop-kicking people with walkers or punting puppies off into the horizon? Are those beliefs as valid as anyone else's?

Just because here in the free world we have the right to free speech doesn't mean everything we say is right. And just because we have freedom of expression doesn't mean what we're expressing isn't absolutely ridiculous!

The prophet Isaiah said, "Woe to those who call evil good and good evil, who put darkness for light and light for darkness, who put bitter for sweet and sweet for bitter."[16]

For goodness' sake, then, don't move your foot from the things you know to be true, the things that produce good and health for you and yours. Don't abandon those patterns and practices that produce purpose and peace. Don't stop exercising or eating well, don't tell your children it's safe to play with matches or juggle knives.

That state that results from validating every idea is not open-minded: it's confusion.

DON'T GIVE YOUR LIFE TO IRRELEVANT MONUMENTS

THE RUINS OF ROME

---

*No one remembers the former generations,
and even those yet to come will not be
remembered by those who follow them.*

—KING SOLOMON #worldchangerbook

Have you ever been to the Roman Forum?

In case you haven't, I'll tell you about it.

First, I should tell you to call it a forum is to be kind. It's not so much a forum anymore as it is a plaza surrounded by the ruins of several ancient government buildings and monuments.

Picture an ornate museum, stuffed into a giant blender, and the contents poured out on the ground.

But back in the day, I was told, the space was a marketplace, the center of the public sphere. It was really *something*. The backdrop for prestigious and notable events like elections and triumphant military processions and great public speeches. The open-air gallery for statues and monuments that commemorated the great men of its day.

When I was there, I was fascinated by it.

I knelt in the dust and tried to read some of the fragments of stone, attempting to make out any symbols or letters I might recognize, trying to trace the message with the tip of my finger, through centuries of dirt embedded in the engraving.

I clearly didn't have the tools to make sense of it.

But I could feel the weight of what it was meant to be. These once glorious columns and extravagant arches. The money and craft and time vested in the rich rock, the intention of someone trying to instill in the granite or marble or other material the nobility of the people it honored.

I could imagine its unveiling. With trumpets sounding, soldiers marching. The triumphant thrust of a fist in the air, a nation's pride fixated on one spot. A reverent, perhaps bowing audience.

I could wonder at their hopes and dreams for that moment. That this sculpture, made out of the most lasting and expensive materials of the time, would stand—a lasting testament to the greatness of that day.

I asked a few passersby, other tourists, if they knew who had built the monument I was studying, which lies in several pieces, broken fragments, partially embedded in the earth. They shook their heads. They couldn't be sure. Perhaps Napoleon, one girl offered.

Another person said maybe it was Caesar.

I asked some local teenagers who were gathered nearby then. Who, I asked, built these monuments? Who were they built to remember?

Perhaps I asked the wrong teenagers, but these ones couldn't be sure.

"They were built so long ago, I don't know if anyone even knows," they told me.

"It's mostly tourists who hang around here. You might

ask one of them. The locals don't really walk through here much," another added.

I stared a little longer at the columns, broken in five or seven pieces, half-embedded in the ground. And I couldn't help wondering what those who commissioned the monuments would've said had they seen what had happened to their masterpieces. I wondered if it might shift their priorities at all. Whether they, if given the chance to do it over, might reconsider whether the time and energy and money spent immortalizing their own achievements was worth it. Or whether they, if they had known their monuments' future place among a tourist attraction referred to as "ruins," might have decided to spend their time, energy, and talent differently.

Actually it's not true to say I wondered that.

As I stepped over a piece of rubble and watched people doing the "say cheese" tourist snapshots while crouching next to bits of crumbled arches, I was pretty sure I knew the answer.

Perhaps the better question to ask, then, was this: What ridiculous monuments that will one day be rendered completely irrelevant am I giving my life and time to now?

INVEST IN WHAT DEVELOPS YOU

IS COLLEGE WORTH THE
THOUSANDS YOU SPEND ON IT?

———————▶◀———————

Change is the end result of all true learning.

—LEO BUSCAGLIA #worldchangerbook

In the world of mission, we may agonize over what we spend our money and our time on. With lives and souls and causes on the line every day, what is worthy of our precious nickels and dimes?

This question emerged as I attended an event for college students who gathered to hear my friend Bart speak.

After his presentation calling students into passionate service to impoverished and marginalized people, a challenge emerged from the crowd.

"You came to a college and said we should go serve the poor," the student pointed out. "We're all paying tens of thousands of dollars to be here, money that could do a lot of good for the poor. Tell me honestly, do you think we should quit school and put the money toward helping the poor?"

Bart smiled a little then, but after a brief pause for thought, he answered.

"The only way you should invest that kind of money in college," he said, "is if you devote yourself to learning. You should only do it if it really develops you beyond where you are now. If these years help you become that much more efficient and prepared and determined, that one day where you would've helped a thousand people, you help ten thousand instead."

I've never thought about time or money or energy the same way since.

WHAT YOU REALLY VALUE

TIME, MONEY, AND ENERGY

———————✕———————

*The outer conditions of a person's life will
always be found to reflect their inner beliefs.*
—JAMES ALLEN #worldchangerbook

What do you really value?

I mean really, down deep, genuinely value?

Before you say anything or think anything, I'll tell you without you saying a word.

In fact, if you say anything, it just might throw me off the scent.

Because most of us say we value things that, as it turns out, we don't really value. So dissecting our words isn't the way to see where our day-to-day allegiance lies.

I'll tell you what you value much more simply than that.

You value (1) Whatever you're putting the most time into and (2) Whatever you're putting the most money into and (3) Whatever you're putting the most energy into.

That's what you value.

And here's an insight that follows closely behind that. Anytime your life gets out of whack, it's a pretty good bet you're putting one of those three things in the wrong place.

WHAT IS NEW DOES NOT ALWAYS TURN OUT TO BE GOOD

SYNONYM FOR GOOD

Be not astonished at new ideas; for it is well known to you that a thing does not therefore cease to be true because it is not accepted by many.

—BARUCH SPINOZA #worldchangerbook

Consider:

New is *not* a synonym for useful.

New is not a synonym for better.

New is not a synonym for relevant.

Sometimes what is new turns out to be good. But it could just as easily be bad.

And even if it once was good, all that was ever sparkly and shiny eventually becomes bland and familiar. What once swooned with momentum eventually plateaus.

Everything new gets old.

Today's new is just tomorrow's old.

You probably have no problem accepting these statements when you pause to reflect on them. But in our culture, these realities tend to get buried. We tend to admire people who are on the "cutting edge" of their fields, those early adopters who are the first to own the latest gadget or the first to clue into a newly discovered pop star.

But new can also be empty. New can be pointless.

Take how the lure of new sometimes manifests in the faith arena.

How when some new idea or new technology emerges in culture, some leaders and churches will race to grab hold of it. They pledge to be the first to get on board and not the last. They refuse to be the bogged down, lumbering old institutional church who is always slogging along a hundred years behind the rest of the culture.

That single that just hit the top Billboard charts? You'll hear it in the preservice playlist the next Sunday morning.

The latest number one comedy? You can count on a video clip of this week's episode as this Sunday's sermon illustration.

The newest handheld gadget? That's the thing the pastor is reading his sermon notes from.

The newest method? The simple church? The missional church? The fluid church? The organic church? We get pre-release copies of the books. We go to the corresponding workshops and conferences. The authors have been to our church to speak twice this year.

We become like the retail industry, enticing people with a church culture of new, new, new. Until it can get to the point where we feel like we have to be new to survive.

This is why, on several occasions, veteran leaders who want to stay relevant to younger generations have asked me, "Should we invest in the newest technology? In swirling graphics and videos embedded behind our song lyrics? Should we have strobe lights? Fog? Scent machines? Multiscreen options?"

Translation.

"Should we always do new things? Should we always buy new equipment? Should we always chase whatever is new in culture? Do you recommend being as new as possible?"

I always give them a qualified yes or a qualified no.

I can say yes, you should adopt technology *if* it helps to advance your purpose. If it makes your mission stronger. If it makes you more effective.

Or I can say no, you should not adopt new technology *unless* it serves your vision, unless it drives home your message, unless it reaches the unreachable.

Their reaction, which I described in the first edition of my first book, *Dear Church*, is often relief. "Oh good." They happily sigh, eased to know that in my book every trend does not require mandatory participation. "Because having those moving images swirling in the background, while a video plays on the alternate screen, while the strobe light flashes above gives us a headache."

"That is exactly the point!" I say. "It gives young people a headache too."

Isn't it terrible that we've gotten to the point that we'd rather induce an auditorium full of headaches than forgo something new?

Use screens when they're useful.

Use lights when they create focus.

Use video when it drives home the purpose.

Use gadgets or social networks when it helps you get important information to people who want it.

But don't use screens for the sake of using screens. Don't install lights for the sake of having lights. Don't put in video for the sake of having videos. Don't buy a gadget or join a social network because you saw it featured in *Wired, Gizmodo,* or *Fast Company.*

If you heard elephants were the newest thing in church props, would you have one imported? Would you put it up on the stage on a platform? Tuck it into the corner with its own little light system and soundtrack? Make up a few hats with trunks and ears? Sell peanuts at the door?

Then you really would have exactly what you might already have now.

Really new elephants that nobody likes, that don't serve your purpose but take up time and energy and space. Elephants that nobody talks about. New elephants in the room.

WHAT IS OLD DOES NOT ALWAYS HAVE TO BE BAD

STRIVING TO BE GOOD ENOUGH TO BE CALLED OLD

———————— ✖ ————————

There are no new ideas.
There are only new ways of making them felt.

—AUDRE LORDE #worldchangerbook

The beautiful part about not seeing new as synonymous with good is that it also infers that old cannot be synonymous with bad either.

And this frees us from being so reactionary. From distancing ourselves from the church of our parents, from adding taglines to our Sunday morning spiels that declare our brand of worship "isn't your grandmother's church."

You like that hymn written in the 1800s? Then sing it! You think pews add majesty to a sanctuary? Then build them anew! You want to have a potluck with casseroles and gravy fountains? Send those parishioners home full!

You want to break away from the mini-value-meal of communion with the Chiclet-sized wafer and thimbleful of Welch's and cook a feast with a roast and big browned loaves of fresh baked bread to break with family and friends? Cook your heart out.

It frees us from the arrogance of thinking our generation

is the one who *finally* got it right, unlike those flawed, imperialistic, capitalistic, sinful, boring, outdated eras of people who went before us. It frees us from thinking the way we use candles on our stage, the props we build, the new curriculum we use, the new social media campaign—that this is the height of faith or well doing. That we, our group among our generation, stand here alone as discoverers of *real* religion or *real* genius, that we have single-handedly ushered in the climax of religious or humanitarian history.

It frees us from the arrogance of believing that our ideas are the only ones that are so unique, so genuine, so organic that they cannot and will not become institutionalized.

And it allows us to marvel and appreciate the richness of a faith passed down from ancients. A timeless, antique faith that has survived many before us and will stretch to survive many beyond us. A faith that is sacred and stable, enduring, but is still internalized and embodied in new ways with each generation.

Which is more awe-striking? More reliable? A new take on faith that emerged yesterday, which packs stadiums at their concerts or conferences? Or a faith that is unwavering, which has survived the best and worst moments of history, the rise and falls of movements and the births and deaths of powerful leaders.

The best stuff of faith, at its core, does not become more or less relevant with each Microsoft update or Apple product that comes out.

Perhaps, then, your grandmother and her church had it right all along.

Perhaps if we really wanted to be doing something valuable with our lives, we would aspire to develop ideas that will survive long enough to be called old by the generations that come after us.

A LITTLE TRICK FOR
FIGURING OUT WHAT MATTERS

FIFTY YEARS FROM NOW

———————————✖———————————

*If you want to test your memory, try to recall
what you were worrying about one year ago.*

—E. JOSEPH COSSMAN #worldchangerbook

I don't know what those sacred people do or think.

Those people who embody God, who recycle peace again and again every day, who stand up and say, All is well. All is well, when the world falls down around them.

You best go to the desert fathers for that one.

Because all I've got is this.

You know that drama? That broiling, infested, achy sick drama that has hold of your life right now? That's sucking your attention, energy, lifeblood?

You know that obstacle? That problem, that barrier, that lack of this or that, that is currently in your way?

You know that enemy? The one who carries themselves with a poison that seeps into your pores, churns acid in your gut, and grates at your soul?

You know that fame? That spotlight, that name up in lights, that this of the year or that of the year, that top ten whatever?

Ask yourself this:

In ten, twenty, thirty, forty, even fifty years, how much will it matter?

Will your elderly self be obsessed with worry about this? Or when you're aged or dead, does that problem, or person, or fame, lose its life too?

There are a few things, the things you hold closest in the deepest parts of your heart, that sustain meaning. Some cause, some barrier, some thing, it is crucial. It is timeless. It is made of the same fabric God works into every generation.

Every era could fight for it and it would still be right.

Every person could invest in it and it would still be worthwhile.

But for many, I'll even say for most things that rivet us today, when we're buried in the ground, and our children or grandchildren are bringing flowers to our grave, trying to live out the principles we have left to them, they probably won't matter at all.

And, truth be told, that's probably about as much as most of them matter now too.

SHOULD I PROMOTE MY OWN WORK AND PROJECTS?

WOULD YOU GROW A TREE AND NOT PICK THE FRUIT?

———————◆———————

Work willingly at whatever you do, as though you were working for the Lord rather than for people.

—THE APOSTLE PAUL #worldchangerbook

Bloggers and aspiring writers occasionally ask me, "Do you think it's okay to promote my stuff on social networks or is that selfish and self-absorbed?"

What can we do? they want to know. What is right?

I've asked the same questions about similar opportunities many times. Enough that I'm not sure a singular answer that would be right for every person in every circumstance exists. But if one does exist, I'll come clean right now by telling you I'm sure I don't have it.

But I will give you a thought to consider.

In most cases, it probably doesn't make sense to invest your time and energy in producing some kind of project and then *not* to promote it.

If you created it in the first place, you probably believed in it, right? Maybe it even came out of God stirring your soul, nurturing the idea along until you couldn't help but bring it to expression. Maybe it represents the best of what you've ever learned. Maybe it holds the deepest of your convictions. Maybe you even believe the principles contained in it could change a person's life!

If this is true, if this is even anywhere near true, then how could you not tell people the project exists?

You believe you are called to be a good steward of what God gives you, right? Doesn't this include your ideas and opportunities?

If it came out of the passion and direction God stirs in you, then do you think God would have to think long about whether he would rather have five people know about it and benefit from it or five thousand?

Let's say your passion and purpose and grooming has led you to plant a fruit tree and that you've spent years reading about trees, studying trees, and learning to grow fruit. Then one day, the tree is full of fruit. What does God want you to do with it?

If you knew other people who needed fruit and still others who really want to plant their own trees, do you think there's much chance—in light of all the opportunity God has allowed around your fruit tree—that he would like you to stop watering yours? Do you think he wants you to take it out of the sunlight? Or to stop fertilizing it?

To not let anyone know it exists?

To just let that fruit shrivel up and die while people around you go hungry?

No, of course not!

God would likely want you to give that tree every possibility of success that you could. To let it benefit as many people as possible.

God's will is for all that belongs to him to bear fruit.

THE IMPORTANCE OF CHECKING YOUR HEART

THE PRAYER OF EXAMEN

The most efficient way to live reasonably is every morning to make a plan of one's day and every night to examine the results obtained.

—ALEXIS CARREL #worldchangerbook

St. Ignatius lived in the 1500s. Depending on if and where you grew up on the Christian spectrum, his name may or may not have crossed your religious radar.

Ignatius was a knight and noble who went on to be a priest and theologian and founded the Society of Jesus (also known as the Jesuits). But of course I don't mention him to deliver a history lesson but to offer a habit I have drawn from his life and writings.

It is called the Prayer of Examen.

You can look into it more if you're interested, but for now, I'll just give you the short and sweet version.

The Prayer of Examen begins with a portion called "Presence." All this means is when you begin to pray, you try to recognize and tune into the presence of God. That you try to remember, even bask in, God's desire to be with you.

The second portion of the prayer is summarized by the word "Gratitude." During this time, one allows his or her mind to drift back over the previous twenty-four hours and to identify what events, people, and things cause them to feel thankful. This is an exercise in recognizing what we have to be grateful about and underlining to ourselves the generosity and goodness of God.

The third portion of this prayer is referred to as "Review." During this time one again looks back over the previous twenty-four hours, but this time, he or she tries to review their actions and notice two things: What parts of the day made you feel like you were aligned most fully with God's desires for your life? And what parts of the day seemed most misaligned? This portion allows us to be aware of how we spend our time and to learn how our past might teach our future.

The final portion of the prayer is termed "Response." This is the time to respond to whatever learning you gathered during the prayer. It is the time to express more gratitude, ask for guidance, or seek help or forgiveness. It is the time to resolve to begin new patterns, to determine how—from this point on—you'd like to live your life differently.

Sounds simple, right? But for me, fair warning, praying this way requires energy and discipline.

Some days, these four processes bring me inspiration and affirmation. I take joy in feeling like my life is finding more and more allegiance with God and his doings. Other days, they can be incredibly discouraging as they remind me just how short I fall in living out the values I am aiming at and just how inconsistent and slow I can be at rooting out behaviors I wish to diminish. But I believe both kinds of days—both the encouraging and the discouraging ones—are valuable to me because they do not allow me to charge forward detached from myself, from others, or from God himself.

I think maybe everyone should give this a go at some point or another.

A LETTER FROM MY SANEST SELF

YOU'RE JUST A MAN

———————✖———————

The best way to test a man's character is to give him power.

—ABRAHAM LINCOLN #worldchangerbook

When I first was offered the contract to publish a book, I was hesitant. I knew that there was good reason to go forward and to hope my own experiences could benefit others, but I was forever marked by having seen others allow fame or recognition, at various levels, disrupt their families, ruin their ministries, and overturn their lives.

Somewhere during that time, I stumbled across a story about Marcus Aurelius who, while ruling Rome, was concerned he might let his power go to his head.

As legend has it, Aurelius hired a servant to literally follow him around as he walked the empire's streets. Every time a citizen bowed a knee or called out a word of praise, Marcus Aurelius instructed the servant to whisper this reminder in his ear: "You're just a man. You're just a man."

Since I was nowhere near this famous and could not afford to hire a person to trail me just to whisper in my ear, I settled for writing a letter that I would never mail but that I would keep in my dresser and refer back to in the future. It was addressed to my future self from my sanest self, and it was a letter from the unknown, un-platformed, off-the-radar me to whatever me I would one day become. And although it touched on a variety of points, it strived to capture the "grounding" I felt in those moments and preserve them as a reminder for any days when my feet might unwisely leave the ground.

It said things like:

Remember the people who helped you get here. Who invested in you on your worst and weakest days, when you had nothing glamorous or noteworthy to offer.

Remember the friends who stood with you in ordinary days, who stood in your kitchen with you at 10:30 at night and made macaroni and cheese. Who drove around in your rusty beater car. And who never needed you to be more than you already were.

Remember that no matter what stage you stand on and no matter who applauds, you are still as deeply human as the next person. You make beds, sort socks, and clean up after dogs nearly every day. This makes you as significant as every other human on the planet and no more so.

I'd wager to say that every person I know might benefit from writing, keeping, and referring back to such a letter, keeping in mind that yours might not be about pride, but it might address some issue that is important to your journey. It might insist to your future self that you believe in yourself, that you put your failures behind you, that you set aside your disabling self-judgment. What will make the letter relevant to you is that it will come from your sanest self and will address parts of your heart that only you and your future self have traveled.

WHEN PEOPLE TRY TO WIN YOUR ALLEGIANCE TO THEIR PET ISSUE

YELL WHERE JESUS YELLED AND WHISPER WHERE JESUS WHISPERED

—◆—

You don't argue with a four-year-old about why he shouldn't eat candy for dinner. . . . It's the path of least resistance. You save your energy for more important battles.

—SCOTT ADAMS #worldchangerbook

There are quite a few things about God, some important, un-moving, foundational things that I think are knowable.

His love for the world, his grace, his decision to send his Son, his desire to redeem us from our own unhealthy and destructive behaviors, his ongoing participation in the world. I could go on, but rather will skip forward in gratitude that this is not a doctoral dissertation, nor am I a denominational official and thus, I don't have to comprehensively develop a creed you all will accept as orthodox.

I cling to these traits revealed in my experience, in the Scriptures, in community, and in my prayer and reflection, as reflective of the enduring nature of God. And in doing so I notice something that you may notice too. What is enough for God is often not nearly enough for people.

I don't mean just people on the theological or political

right and I don't mean just people on the left and I don't mean just people in the center. I mean human beings, in general, get our own hopes and expectations mixed up with God's fairly often.

As a result, in the arena of faith, there will always be people who will want you to focus on issues you see as tangent. They will want you to build your platform and invest your life as a spokesman for something mentioned in a single Old Testament Bible verse because to them this is the pinnacle on which their whole theological worldview tenuously balances.

For them to affirm your God-with-ness, they need you to tip the scale on their pet issue one way or the other. Again, this so often goes for conservatives and liberals alike.

Sometimes rightly so.

In some cases, ethics and morality, and a thorough treatment of the Scriptures let alone obedience to God, our spirit may convict us of the necessity of publicly advocating around any given subject, regardless of whether it be tangent to salvation.

And if this is how your soul instructs you to move, I won't pretend I have a right to take away the freedom of thought and action God himself grants us all by telling you otherwise.

But I will concede there are times where my own sensibilities about God, my own consciousness of His Spirit, my own reading of the Bible, my own take on spiritual tradition, my own survey of community wisdom does not lead me to the brink of the issue that some religious groups demand I stand on. And in case your life ever takes you there, where beings who are not God try to occupy your soul-space and crowd out the voice of God in your life, I offer you this.

There is a finite amount of time and energy available to me. I cannot possibly take on the spiritual burdens or campaigns of every person I know, particularly because many of them hold them in opposition to each other. In living our lives or stating our beliefs, we will often hear boos from half of the gym regardless of what call we make. What I will do, then, is reverence and attribute worth to God and internalize and embody the teachings of Jesus the best I know how. I will, in deference to the parting instructions of Jesus, give preference to expressions of the good news.

But in a lot of other things, I'm going to, and in sometimes I'm even deciding ahead of time to, let you down. Because, as much as I respect you and as often as I even agree with you, my allegiance in this world is not to a set of ideas you'd like me to set up camp around. Nor do I believe the message of the gospel is to live my life as your mouthpiece.

No way. In a whole lot of things, I'm playing the trump card of Savior. I'm choosing to *yell where Jesus yelled and whisper where Jesus whispered.*

Section 7
PASSION & IDENTITY

I wanted to change the world but I have found the only thing one can be sure of is changing oneself.

—ALDOUS HUXLEY #worldchangerbook

WHEN IDENTITY IS MIXED UP IN LIFE

WHEN FRIENDS, CHURCH, AND COWORKERS ARE ONE

———————— ✖ ————————

*To be yourself in a world that is constantly
trying to make you something else
is the greatest accomplishment.*

—RALPH WALDO EMERSON #worldchangerbook

Do you love your life work?

Does your day-to-day job revolve around the stuff you care most about? Is it what you would want to invest your life in whether you got paid or not?

Good for you! A lot of people slogging away making widgets or faxing papers for their paycheck would envy that.

But also tricky for you. Because questions of identity and boundary become that much stickier when your job is embedded in your passions.

In a job in an unrelated field, it might be easier for some of us to stay healthy. It would be a lot harder (but not impossible) for our boss to persuade us to stay until 10 p.m. faxing papers or making widgets. We'd be less willing to give up our free time to staple and make copies to make the CEO's bonus check fatter.

We don't necessarily do these sorts of jobs because the

work is central to who we are or because it is tied up in our identities. We do it because ideally they are tasks we find interesting and we draw a paycheck. We use it to put a roof over our head. To feed ourselves and maybe others. Overtime, in these scenarios then, isn't about making the world a better place, it's about paying our bills, covering the cost of our kids' braces, maybe—in a steady year—buying that gadget or pair of tennis shoes we've been wanting.

In the best-case scenarios in these kinds of jobs, we at least enjoy creating presentations or fashioning parts on an assembly line. Maybe it fits with some skill inside of us. But would we take a bullet for it? Would we sideline the rest of our lives, shortchange our families, and live and breathe for it?

Not so much, right?

But man oh man oh man is working in your passion area more tricky than that.

The work in this specific field is the kind of stuff you dreamed of doing. It's your top choice for how to spend your time. It's the thing you're drawn to, what you wake up every morning wanting to do, it is the thing that delights your soul.

And it's not just about you!

The well-being of other people is attached to those missions and causes—customers, clients, parishioners, recipients of your charitable efforts.

Do you work for a nonprofit that helps indigenous people groups market their wares to make a living? Do you help install clean water wells to prevent communities from contracting cholera? Do you try to find homes for orphans? Do you provide AIDS education? Do you present trainings for teenage moms? Do you speak faith over people who are spiritually unwell?

Well then, your work is important!

No wonder you do it for reasons beyond a paycheck! You do it because God has stirred a conviction inside you, put you on a path. What you are doing supports God's purposes in the world. Your work helps people experience the fullest life possible, and even more so, has eternal weight.

Holy cow! How could you *not* want to sideline everything else, to pour out everything you are, to devote every waking minute and second to that sort of significance, right? And herein lies the problem.

Your faith gets mixed up in your work.

Your identity gets mixed up in your work.

Your worth gets mixed up in your work.

And that seems fine on the days where things are going well.

Bliss! Bliss! Hardworking, passionate bliss!

But please hear me on this: the more happy you are, sometimes the more you love what you do, the more important you think it is, the easier it is for you to unknowingly wander into unhealthiness.

It can happen.

Your work produces endless lists of things you'd like to do, unending lines of need. It teases you with benchmarks—if I could just raise this amount of money or get this number of people involved, then we'd be humming!

You realize that your cause provides more work than you could possibly do in a thousand lifetimes. But this does not immediately dissuade you. Because this stuff is important!

This is the stuff of your dreams!

As follows, you don't mind clocking a few extra hours here and there. You don't mind carting a boatload of papers home from work. You don't mind having people over to your house at night, or setting up weekend events.

It's for the cause, after all.

At first you think, how great is this that I love my job so much I'm willing to go at it this hard? People are out there who hate their jobs, who wouldn't work a second past five even to double their salary.

How lucky I am to want to do this day after day after day after day!

But then this is where the trickiness begins.

Because after enough days pile up, our bodies start to feel the strain of those long hours and heavy concentration. We wake up tired. Our families or friends feel a little bit neglected. Some household chores get skipped.

Yet we keep going. When our cause is this important, it's worth a little strain on the energy level. Our families and friends understand. A few dirty dishes aren't nearly as important as spirituality, as orphans, as health care.

And we go along like that for a while. Sacrifice, sacrifice, sacrifice.

Until we're so weary we don't really want to do it any longer. We begin to wonder if it's worth it. We fear our pace is destructive and we can't keep going.

And that's when we realize: we set a trap for ourselves and walked right in it.

We killed it in the beginning. We told ourselves this was a temporary "extra-busy" stretch. That this was crunch time.

The night before finals. We poured ourselves in, day in and day out, trying to create momentum, to get things ramped up. This was to be the storm before the calm.

And we succeeded! Things are moving! We've got things humming! More people are caring every day! The organization is growing!

And . . . so are the responsibilities of maintaining it.

Now we've got everything flying along at 90 mph, and we were expecting we'd get past this stage somehow, that things would settle in and we'd just coast for a while. That we'd go back to our families, clean our houses, go to movies again.

But that's not what happened.

Now that things are going along at Mach speed, we feel obligated to keep up the productivity. We've created more need, more growth, more tasks . . . all of which seem good because they expand the mission.

We can't stop. If we do, balls we've been juggling will fall to the floor. Things won't get done. People won't be served.

But we don't stop. We don't allow ourselves to wake up. Why? Because we believe in sacrificing for what we believe in. We believe in pouring ourselves out. In giving everything we have. At being drained at the end of the day, knowing we expended all the resources we had to give.

And suddenly, we feel pressured. If we stop, we will let other people—and ourselves—down.

But we can't stop because our faith is mixed up in it.

Somewhere along the way, we stopped being a world changer and became a martyr.

The person whose life has been changed most is our own. And it's changed in the wrong direction. Now we are slaves to our cause. We have no freedom, no options.

Stop the madness.

Pull back—you have to!

You've come to believe a lie. You've come to believe your vision can't survive unless you exhaust yourself over it. But the complete opposite is actually true. Your vision can't survive unless you *stop* exhausting yourself over it.

Are you already performing less than the best in everything you do? Are you letting everyone in your life down just a little? Are you so full of tasks and people that you've stopped feeling, that you have to numb yourself to continue on? Have you stopped loving sharing the work you're doing? Are you just giving unplugged, checked-out presentations? Is the passion and sparkle gone from your eyes?

Then stop already!

Stop and recalibrate.

Take back your identity.

You are not your job.

You are not your cause.

You are not your mission.

You are still you even without any of that.

Take back your worth.

You have value outside your job.

Outside your cause.

Outside your mission.

Reverse this crazy idea you have in your head that if you run yourself dry, you have given the most. You will give the world the most if you'll still be alive and healthy enough to serve tomorrow.

You are more good to the world well.

NO ONE GETS TO OWN YOUR FAITH

REFUSE TO LOOK THROUGH JUST ONE LENS AT GOD

———————✕———————

I am not bound to please thee with my answer.
—WILLIAM SHAKESPEARE #worldchangerbook

No human being or groups of beings should ever get to own your faith.

Please. Write that down.

Christian tradition and your faith community—along with your reading of the Bible, intellect, and prayer life—provide valuable feedback.

But no individual or group gets to own or control your faith.

Not your local church. Not your nonprofit or company or other place of work. Not your association or denomination. Not some Christian movement or camp of thinkers. Not even your mentor or your parents or your siblings or your children.

All of these groups and people may be a wonderful source of wisdom and by all means, don't dismiss them. Give them a fair hearing. Consult them and seek to apply the wisdom they offer.

But at the end of the day, when it comes to your soul

and how you invest your life and express your faith, the buck stops with you.

If you let them talk you into a certain career, a certain set of doctrines, a certain expression of faith, they will not be the one who will live the results of those choices. They will not be accountable for you. They will not weather your failures or take responsibilities for your mistakes. They will not and cannot stand between you and how God feels about those decisions. Whatever path you take, and whatever good or bad follows, they are yours and yours alone. Be sure these decisions gel with your own conscience!

The best leaders and organizations in our lives acknowledge this. They share all the wisdom and learning they've offered to help us understand the benefit of their advice or ideas, but respect that God himself gave you the ability to think freely and do not try to take away a freedom God himself does not rescind.

Good leaders realize that if they did this, it would cease to be shepherding and cross over into control. That it would short-circuit your journey or might spoon-feed you into adopting something you don't really believe and excuse you from absorbing and owning God's truths for yourself.

Think about it.

If a person or organization tells you, *you must only look at God through the lens I am giving you,* if they say, *you must only read the Scriptures looking for the conclusions I have given,* they would be putting themselves in between you and God.

Instead they should be saying what Paul said: Test all things![1] Take every new idea before God. Weigh it against what you know of him and his truths.

Search God out for all he is willing to reveal himself to be. Learn everything you can about him, experience as many facets of him as you can. I will not try to stand between you and what God may be doing in your life, nor will I try to prevent you from learning some of the things I already have on your own. I will not tell you to stop your own exploration, even if it proves different from how God has worked in my own life. There is already a go-between to mediate between you and God and it is not me. So closely guard your motives, heed the movement of the Holy Spirit, and take my blessings as you live your own adventure with God.

The day we let humans—even the polished, educated, churchgoing—occupy the space between us and God, the day we let them direct our thinking or talk us into positions that go against our own conscience, we commit idolatry. We take back our allegiance to God and we give it to something that is less than God.

Anger is like gasoline. If you spray it around and somebody lights a match, you've got an inferno. But if we can put our anger inside an engine it can drive us forward.

—SCILLA ELWORTHY #worldchangerbook

DESIRES OF YOUR HEART

WHAT PSALM 37 DOESN'T SAY

———————— ✖ ————————

A shortcut to riches is to subtract from our desires.

—PETRARCH #worldchangerbook

If you've ever been hopeful God would grant some request, intervene in some circumstance, provide some miracle solution, you have probably stumbled across a verse that made you hopeful. Something like Psalm 37:3–4, which says God will "give you the desires of your heart."

Yes! The wanting parts of ourselves cry. *Look, there it is in black-and-white. God wants to be my fairy godmother. He wants to wave his wand when I wish upon a star. God, we plead, I know your Word says you want to give me the desires of my heart . . . so lay* fill-in-the-blank *on me!*

But, but, but. Most of us have realized the verse isn't the rainbow to our pot of gold. Or at least, if it is, the gold hasn't turned up yet.

But before we dismiss this one, go back. What does it say?

"Trust in the Lord," the psalm says, "and do good; dwell in the land and enjoy safe pasture. Take delight in the Lord, and he will give you the desires of your heart."

Trust in the Lord.

Take delight in him.

And as you are doing so, he will give you the desires of your heart.

Wait, this can't be right. That makes it seem like some secret, hidden formula for getting God on board with our Christmas list.

But consider this: What happens as you trust in the Lord? You gain perspective. You begin to see your life in terms of God's economy. Things that seemed risky may seem safe. Steps you were too lazy, afraid, or unable to take may open up before you.

You see new things in new ways.

And very likely based on this new vision you acquire, you will begin to want new things in new ways as well.

What happens, then, as we delight in the Lord? As we happily take on his intentions? The desires of our heart begin to shift. Our desires become more like his desires. What we want for the world becomes more like what he wants for the world.

And we, as we trust, as we delight, suddenly are looking at the circumstances in front of us, we are bearing God into them, seeing what he sees in them, wanting what he wants for them, our hearts are crying out for his desires.

This is how he gives us the desires of our heart.

But wait, you protest. It's a trick. This means God never has to give me that A-list celebrity for a spouse! He never has to UPS a cool $3 million to my door. He could entirely ignore my original wish list.

No, no, no.

What a sad thing this would be to conclude. That would miss the point altogether.

It isn't that God ignores your wish list. It's that *you* ignore your wish list. Because suddenly God is helping you revise that list of things you've been wanting, and in the place of fake and fraudulent things you were wanting, he gives you things that will make you more happy, stable, gracious, at peace, wiser than you ever were smart enough to ask for.

Stop fearing that God wants to harm you!

We have to stop thinking that we, in our smartest, most genius moves, might be able to manipulate a better end than what God can.

That we might just be a little smarter than God . . . that he just might not see that if he gave us that grand mission, that noble way of life, that full soul *and a million dollars and made us impervious to sickness and disease,* it would be just right.

He's not giving us less than what we asked for, he's giving us more.

He's shaping us to set our eyes and heart on the things that will bring us well-being not just today but tomorrow, the next day, and for all time.

He's helping us ask for what will stir good for us and our world not just in our present location and time and emotion, but no matter where we are, when we are, who we are with, or what is happening to us.

Yes, he's the good God who doesn't give us a stone when we ask for bread.

But he's also the good God who may not hand us one flimsy cup of sugary, caffeinated pop when we insist we're thirsty. He's the God of living water who takes us to the faucet, where water streams all day and all night, where we can drink as much as we want from what's good for us.

FREEDOM FROM A TYRANT

THE MONEY THAT IMPRISONS US

———————————— ⋈ ————————————

There is nothing wrong with men possessing riches.
The wrong comes when riches possess men.
—BILLY GRAHAM #worldchangerbook

Advertisements are everywhere.

They're still on TV, in the newspapers, in magazines, same as always. They're on T-shirts and in website banners and sidebars. But they've also taken up new residence. They're played before movies at the theater now. They're in your mailbox, on subways, in baseball parks, on the coffee cup at a conference. They're in the personalized Gmail and Facebook ads, in text-linked ads in an article, on custom-detailed cars, in your Amazon recommendations. They're in bathroom stalls, for Pete's sake.

Why? Are companies just trying to get their logos and products on any surface they can? Well, yes of course. It's a fight for visibility. They'd screen print or digitally deliver an ad inside the lenses of your sunglasses if they could. They'd place implant devices in your ears to whisper sweet nothings of subliminal messages 24/7. Or they'd skip all that and upload the data into your brain if you only had a USB port.

Don't think they wouldn't buy billboard space in your dreams if they could figure out how.

No way, you say. *That's a fine analogy and all, but I'd never let someone hardwire ads into my brain! It would be too annoying to have to ignore all that product flashing before my senses, to weed it all out and see the things I actually want to look at.*

Yes exactly—you're on to something!

If we wouldn't let them do that, then why do we let them lure us in now? To plaster our environment with the next miracle product—that one tube or bottle of whatever that really *does* eliminate vehicle rust, melt off 20 pounds overnight, whiten our teeth, or vanquish gray hair forever? To lure us into buying *yet another* temporary, empty promise—to sit half-used under our sink and in our drawers and closets.

If we're really so adamant that these people don't get to control how we process our lives, then stand up to it!

Unclutter your storage. Be able to open your closet without things falling out, close your junk drawer without it getting caught, and empty the space under your bed.

How did we ever become convinced that needing a bed skirt to hide junk we store on the floor was a good idea?

Who sold us on the idea that it is a good practice to keep a *junk* drawer? So we'll always have junk on hand? Good gracious, we would not want to live without junk at our fingertips.

What about those multi-item hangers that stand in your closet? Those vacuum compacted containers? Those clever shoe organizers that hang on anything with an edge? Now instead of holding on to ten pairs of pants we never wear, we can store a hundred pairs we'll never use. How convenient! Now instead of five pairs of pants, we can have fifty. What progress!

This is where we must take back our field of vision.

Cast off thought control and fight for our freedom.

Because that's what it is, you know—we may have fought our revolution for independence long ago. But a lot of us gave up our freedom for a new tyrant: consumerism.

You say, wait, isn't this a bit exaggerated?

I hope so.

But think about it!

How much time do we spend accumulating possessions only to then have to maintain them? How many clothes do we buy just to wash and dry them, iron or dry-clean them, fold and store and sort through them when we need something to wear? How much money do we spend buying containers to house them—little plastic and cardboard apartments and condos for our clothing. And then upgrading them to bigger containers and closets, to crawl spaces and attics. Here, have a house in your own gated community, little clothes. A neighborhood all for you, my dear shoes.

How much time do we spend acquiring a place to live only to preserve it? How many hours do we devote to sweeping and dusting and decluttering never thinking that an extra thousand square feet directly correlates to the time we have available to read books or take in nature or hug children? How much energy do we devote to choosing the right color paints and patterns, a knickknack here and there? To reading home magazines and watching HGTV?

It's never ending!

How much energy do we sink into doing endless updating, painting a room only to discover the curtains now look faded next to our bright new walls. Replace the curtain and notice how drab the armchair in front of the window has become in comparison. Replace the kitchen floor only to notice the bathtub needs our attention. It's one room after another, and then when we've completed our first round and are doing our victory lap, we notice a horrifying reality. Something in Room #1 has come undone, worn out, grown outdated. And so we begin again!

It's exhausting to just think about it, isn't it?

Stop the madness!

Where you live becomes not a home but a time-sucker!

There's a funny reality when it comes to money. Sometimes people don't need to break into your house to take your possessions. Sometimes, when you keep those possessions, you rob yourself of just as much, especially when you may be keeping them at the expense of your sanity, your freedom, or your ability to rest and enjoy life.

Sometimes even when you're feasting during a famine, the real person who is starving is you.

THE GIFT OF DISILLUSIONMENT

THE ORIGIN OF "DISILLUSION"

———————✖———————

When written in Chinese, the word crisis *is composed of two characters. One represents danger and the other represents opportunity.*

—JOHN F. KENNEDY #worldchangerbook

Has someone or something let you down?

Have they ruined all your hopes and dreams about some part of life? Have they shattered your expectations?

Are you now disoriented, not sure you can trust the things you once did? Must you now rethink everything?

Good.

I know that doesn't sound compassionate, but I mean it with all love. I really do.

Are you disillusioned? That is absolutely wonderful!

If you can only see the bad in it, quick, you must stand everything on its head and look at it again! Here is the insight you must look for: Disillusionment does not have to be a setback. It can be an opportunity.

It's true. I didn't even make that up. It's in the very definition of the word.

The prefix "dis"? It means "away from."

And "illusion"? Well that means a "false impression of reality."

To be disillusioned, then, is *to move away from a false impression of reality.*

That means, to be disillusioned is to unmask the lies. To keep searching and keep learning beyond what we believed we knew yesterday and look forward to all God might be willing to reveal to us in the future.

WHAT TO DO WITH ANONYMOUS CRITICS

HATE MAIL THAT IS SIGNED BY NOBODY . . .

———————— ✖ ————————

A successful man is one who can lay a firm foundation with the bricks that others throw at him.

—SIDNEY GREENBERG #worldchangerbook

I remember someone once saying there are two kinds of critics: the ones who confront you directly, and the ones who come after you anonymously.

Here is my advice for the latter:

Invite your critic to identify themselves, enter into relationship with you, and voice their criticism within the context of that relationship.

Insist on humanizing each other via a phone call, a Skype conversation, a personal encounter . . . or at the very least, via a signed email and contact information.

They probably won't take you up on it.

And if they don't offer you that grace, of treating you humanely and acknowledging your personhood, then that tells you exactly what to do with their feedback. Treat it like a robot accidentally misfired and errantly sent you a message based on the wrong information.

Several peers who write and speak have passed on to

me this same word of wisdom: Hate mail signed by no one is from no one.

Or as I sometimes add, if your critics choose to be invisible, let them have their wish.

VULNERABLE BULLIES

WHEN DEALING WITH
INJURED CHILDREN . . .

———————✖———————

To avoid criticism do nothing, say nothing, be nothing.
—ELBERT HUBBARD #worldchangerbook

So your critics.

There's a chance that they are stellar people. That they have sacred insides and holy bearings. That they are keyed in to God. Attuned to his stirrings in the universe.

They may just be those rare, solid sorts of people. The kind who can simultaneously believe in you, and hold allegiance to you, even when they disagree with you. The kind who have the personal courage to debate you, to push back on you, who don't allow you to dismiss or dissuade them with ease. The kind who put in the time to know you and be known by you, who take the credible route of making you certain of their allegiance, and who are willing to pay the cost of uncomfortable conversations to give you genuine support and not just unending displays of approval.

If so, good for you.

Seek them out. Invite them to reveal their honest take on where you're at and what you're doing. Trust them. Let them save you from your own flaws and protect you from the consequences of missteps.

Can you imagine? If another human being could save you days, weeks, months, maybe even years of suffering or hardship? If they were kind enough to stand in the way of you and hurt or to lodge themselves between you and failure?

Put a bow on that in your conscience and call it what it is—a gift!

Use and cherish it. Assume God believes what you're doing is important enough to give you such a measured and intentional person, a deeper support than what many in this world will ever experience.

But let's not act like this is the norm. A lot of the criticisms we take in this world come from a different place and are moved by a different spirit.

Sometimes these critics will bear truth, but they bear it with weaponry that only gets to your insides because they stab you so many times to get there.

How do you hear their assessment? Do you grit your teeth, suck it up, and let someone have at the deepest and most important movements of your heart? The most significant experiences, learnings, or facets of your identity?

How do you live with that? How do you not let it derail your mission or sideline you in sadness or disappointment?

May I suggest you put their authority to give criticism into context?

That you immediately insist on treating them as who they are?

A human being.

A possibly flawed, self-appointed human being.

That you remind yourself they cannot disturb your peace, they cannot cast some spell over you that thrusts you into negative emotional cycles.

They are not, it is sometimes helpful to remember, an authority on all of life or the condition of the human heart. Their opinions are not representative of all mankind.

They have not been assigned the task of weighing the motives of souls.

They're a lot less powerful than that.

They are a lot more vulnerable, and more threatened than that.

They've experienced joy and warmth the same way you have. But they've also experienced suffering or loss. They've celebrated friendships and grieved relationships gone bad. Disease and death have robbed them of people they loved. Sin and dysfunction have damaged their lives, delivered them failures, broken their marriages, disappointed their supporters. They have failed. They've been wounded and unhealthy. In fact, they might very well be injured and sick right now.

And if so, you cannot trust the words of one in such agony.

It may be difficult to take their sting and not vilify them. To not allow your mind the luxury of finding nothing valid or admirable about them or what they say.

But the truth is, they are a mix. Just like you and me.

They didn't grow up wanting to bully you. If they bully, it's likely that something went severely wrong in their own development. People failed to be to them what they needed when they needed it. And as a result, they function in some ways as underdeveloped preemies trying to breathe and function in a world meant for someone stronger and healthier.

And this is where they lose their power to harm you but not their humanity or voice.

A weak and injured child can warrant our compassion rather than our judgment. They can tap supernatural reservoirs of grace. Remind yourself every hater, every enemy, every critic was once likely that child. It may just free you to look on them with the eyes of Jesus and believe that who they have become is a sad outcome given the fullness God had intended for them.

And therefore, to receive and respond in grace.

ENDLESS WORRYING HELPS NO ONE

A FIVE-MINUTE LIMIT

―――――――――――⬛―――――――――――

Worry does not empty tomorrow of its sorrow.
It empties today of its strength.

—CORRIE TEN BOOM #worldchangerbook

Here is a quick and easy trick to limiting the impact of worry and frustration, or of most bad feelings in general.

Hold yourself to a five-minute per day limit.

What that person did to you. What that camp has said or believed about you. How this or that place or person is failing you.

Five minutes. Think it over. Try to get to the bottom of it. Pray it up. Try to eagle eye a solution.

Then cut yourself off.

Refuse to give any bad more than a few minutes of your time. You have not pledged allegiance to forces that harm you. You do not owe them your whole day. You do not owe them a good night's sleep. You owe them nothing!

Do not allow those who seek to harm you or experiences that have weighed you down to take control of more than five minutes. Stake your personal flag, bearing the crest of Jesus, in the rest of your life and claim it for what you do live for. Don't give up that mental territory.

Take those thoughts captive.

Sure, there might be some guiding conversations that you have with mentors or loved ones that help you plunge the depths of your soul looking for wisdom or healing. But when you've said all you've had to say and heard out the voices you respect, then stop talking about it.

Don't let ill will dominate more than five minutes of your conversation. Vent, self-express, but don't indulge. Don't go deep-sea diving in the Mariana Trench of all that's wrong. Speak it out loud if necessary. *Phew, I got that out of my system, but I promised myself I wouldn't give my energy to things that subtract from my life.*

But hardship isn't just inflicted by a person, you say. It's the nature of life itself. It's grief, it's loss.

Yes, the world hurts and skews things so bad sometimes. Still.

Five minutes.

What does worrying more than that accomplish? If something is deep inside you so bad, if it's scarred you and wrecked you, it's probably outside your control. Is it not?

So if you had to choose between investing five minutes of your life that will accomplish nothing, and hours upon hours that will accomplish nothing, which do you choose?

For the good of all, if you insist on wasting more than five minutes of your time doing something that accomplishes nothing, then at least put the time into some sort of nothingness that's enjoyable.

Stare off into the ocean, lose yourself in the blue sky, wander off in the planets. Breathe deeply.

Time is finite. It's the one thing we all wish we had

more of. It should be among the resources we steward most astutely.

It's poor caretaking to permit your mind and mouth to waste your time and energy. So again, we set our minds on things that are good, noble, and of well report. Once more, we calibrate ourselves to good things.[1]

POWERLESS WORDS AREN'T WORTH SAYING

SOMETIMES IT'S BETTER TO BE HEARD THAN TO BE RIGHT

---◆---

Great thoughts speak only to the thoughtful mind,
but great actions speak to all mankind.

—THEODORE ROOSEVELT #worldchangerbook

Talking.

For some of us, it's a tool for learning. It's processing out loud. It's inviting synchronicity. It's formulating and firming up ideas.

It feels inherently productive just to have got our idea outside of our tanks of bodies where they've been swimming around.

We find success in just getting it expressed.

But here's the thing about talking.

It's only valuable to the degree it can be heard.

You can give twenty minutes of the world's most inspiring speech, packed full of illustrations and metaphors and heartfelt reasoning that could melt glaciers. But if the person you're talking to checks out 60 seconds in, then the speech never inspires.

The same goes for a lot of things.

Want to speak the truth in love to someone?

Here's the thing. If the person isn't capable of receiving truth in love, then your message never delivers wisdom and it won't communicate affection.

If you drown someone in helpful verbiage, but it doesn't meet the need they're searching for assistance on, then the help falls flat.

Another way of saying this is this: Sometimes it's better to get people to hear love than it is to get people to ignore that you're right.

Section 9
FAITH & EXPECTATIONS

Our generation does not want its epitaph to read,

"We kept charity overhead low."

We want it to read that we changed the world.

—DAN PALLOTTA #worldchangerbook

DON'T OBSESSIVELY LOOK BEYOND WHERE YOU ARE

THE ILLUSION OF SOMEDAY AND SOMEWHERE

———————————▶◀———————————

Remember that happiness is a way of travel,
not a destination.

—ROY GOODMAN #worldchangerbook

Life, as you've likely noticed, isn't perfect.

At any given moment, it might be unfair, hard, and far less than ideal.

Knowing this, we sometimes prefer to check out of the grind and start dreaming about how life might one day be. To live not in today, and not even in the future, but to live in an imagined future called "someday."

Someday is a fictional stretch of time that, if it arrives at all, will only arrive in part. And we create it by telling ourselves that "someday" that perfect job will arise. Maybe when we're done with grad school, when we have the house paid off. When we get that promotion or when the funding comes in. When we have more freedom in our schedule, more followers, more website visitors, more products or CDs or books selling. Then we will have arrived! And we'll experience the climax of our existence that is waiting for us.

But the problem with someday is it might just crowd out today.

It might siphon our best hopes or resources out of the moment we are living and project them onto a day where they may not even be useful, onto a day that is not even guaranteed to us, onto a day that may never come.

Whenever we're tempted to imagine our energies onto a possible, but not certain, future, we might be wise to ask:

What if what God is doing right now is as important as anything I'll ever do? What if the way our life is playing out in this specific moment—this rhythm, this people, this work—is as much what we were born to do as any other activity we'll ever take on? If it is exactly what, through any series of unpredictable circumstances, would make our life count the most?

We often do the same thing with geography. We want to go on a journey to three countries like the author of *Eat, Pray, Love*. We want to take on some adventurous mission work in a foreign country. Exotic languages. Native foods. Crazy stories of cultural interfaces.

But what if somewhere is also an illusion?

What if we have just crafted a faraway fantasy land, projected our hopes onto some location to help us feel better about the monotony or struggle of our current setting? What if we are checking out of there to live in some possible there, one we may never reside in, a make-believe place called "somewhere"?

What if somewhere is a fictional set of latitude and longitude, a place that, if it exists at all, only exists in part. Someday is a fictional stretch of time that, if it arrives at all, will only arrive in part. And we create it by telling ourselves that our cause will arrive in this pretend land of there. When we no longer have the funding barriers we have here. When we no longer have the critics and detractors of here barking in our ears. When we have a city or region or country full of many more supporters than we have here.

There we will have arrived! And we'll experience the climax of our existence that is waiting for us.

In no way am I discrediting international ventures. There is endless good to be done overseas, particularly in acting generously toward struggling communities in the developing world.

But what if where we are now is the best place we will ever be? What if the place where we were born, the place where we were trained, or the place where our work is now in play is the place where we are best suited to serve? The place where we know the language, where we understand the culture, where we have access to networks and an understanding of how to acquire and distribute resources.

What if we were to refuse to rely on the illusion of someday or somewhere and embrace this sort of contentment about today and here. There would perhaps be no greater gift than when you realize the best point of time and the best place to be are right where you are.

IF YOU HAVE TO MANIPULATE TO GET SOMETHING, YOU WILL HAVE TO MANIPULATE TO KEEP IT

THE NEVER-ENDING CYCLE OF DISTORTION

To fake it is to stand guard over emptiness.

—ARTHUR HERZOG #worldchangerbook

Here's a little rule that has served me time and time again.

If you have to manipulate and calculate to "win" someone, you'll have to manipulate and calculate to keep them.

That is pretty much true cross-contexts.

If you have to pretend to be someone you're not to attract a potential spouse, you'll have to continue the charade once you're married.

If you have to swallow your real opinions to earn someone's admiration, you'll have to bury your real perspectives to keep their respect in the future.

If you have to let a leader disacknowledge your contribution in order to be accepted on the team, then you will never be credited or promoted for your efforts.

Our mind sometimes tells us this isn't the case. It suggests somehow manipulation can eventually lead to authenticity. That we will fake it, but then one day we will make it, and we'll be able to cast aside our acting skills later.

But our mind lies.

Manipulation and authenticity can't coexist.

Lies don't lead to truth, only to more lies. Those lies eventually become impossible to sustain, to yourself or to others, and things unravel.

Save yourself the unraveling. Save yourself the emotional struggle. The wasted investment. Live without them peaceably now, and save yourself the trouble of wrenching your life free of them later.

KNOW WHEN SOMEONE CAN'T BE TRUSTED, EVEN IF THE SOMEONE IS YOU

THE COMMON DENOMINATOR

———————————◄►———————————

*Know yourself. Don't accept your dog's admiration as
conclusive evidence that you are wonderful.*

—ANN LANDERS #worldchangerbook

Here's another helpful little hint that has served me well on
more than one occasion: If a person seems to have drama with
everyone, it's only a matter of time until they have drama
with you.

Was every workplace they ever served in out to get them?

Was every person they ever dated inferior?

Is every family member a monster?

Is every old friend a villain?

Every acquaintance a traitor?

Here is when you must return to high school algebra and
call it like it is. The common denominator in the drama is
them.

I'm not saying lose faith. I'm not saying abandon them.
I'm not saying don't find the deepest, most enduring grace
that you can muster.

I'm just saying don't be sidelined. Don't choose them as

your confidant or count on them to be part of your forever. And don't stand there shocked out of your mind when they get angry at you or your relationship falls apart.

If they came for their bosses, if they came for their co-workers, if they came for their exes, family, friends, sooner or later they'll be coming for you.

And one more thing: when you do the hard math, and boil all the previous situations down to the lowest common denominator, you may find the mole that you're hunting for is you!

If so, don't dismay. Don't waste time dramatizing it. Protecting it. Denying it.

Be glad you found out sooner than later. This means you can save yourself all kinds of future trouble.

If you find you are the saboteur, then this is good news. For this is the very saboteur who you have the potential to change the most.

WE TEND TO BE QUICK TO BLAME OTHERS

YOU'RE REALLY MAD AT YOURSELF FOR BEING WRONG

———◆———

Informed decision making comes from a long tradition of guessing and then blaming others for inadequate results.

—SCOTT ADAMS #worldchangerbook

I wonder if this has happened to you as many times as it's happened to me.

You've met some new person and thought, *I like her. I admire him. I think this person will bring good to my life.*

You've come into some group and thought, *This is a great place. I like being here. This is going to contribute to my well-being.*

You've had some opportunity, some experience that you thought, *This is it! This is a great find. I'm going to love this. What's coming is going to be deeply satisfying.*

But then somewhere along the way, things went a different direction. Your opinions and judgments were completely disturbed.

Maybe a relationship or an experience fizzled. Maybe the other parties just weren't as committed or into it as you were.

Maybe something bad went down. Maybe it ended in pain or betrayal or disappointment.

Your mind takes all this data, punches it into your calculator, and comes to a quick answer.

These people let me down.

They misled me.

They didn't come through.

And then the sadness about that, the loss of quality in the relationship or the damaged mutual respect really comes back to you. Maybe you don't dwell on it day and night, but when it does come up, it brings you a bad feeling.

Maybe, in the worst cases, it even affects the way you relate to others in the future.

Maybe it makes you less trusting.

Less likely to dig into community.

Maybe, over time, the repetition of turnabouts like this severely lowers your expectations for those around you, for experiences . . . for even life in general.

I'll tell you how I sideline, or at least shorten, those bouts of disappointment. Because it's really helped me. Opened up the world to me almost.

But it's not easy advice to swallow. Nor is it easy to implement.

And you won't like it.

Nevertheless, here's where you have to reframe the moment. It's in that space where disappointment strikes, that stretch of time where you become conscious that someone or something has failed to become what you expected.

And this is what you must say to yourself.

This is my doing.

I'm the one who made a judgment about who she was. A judgment that turned out to be mistaken.

I tried to cast him in a role different than the one he really plays in this world. Or, I expected her to respond in a way that reflected who I wanted her to be rather than who she truly is.

I wrote a script he didn't have a copy of.

She didn't get to read my invisible manual.

So the party I have to blame for my failed expectations? It's not those who didn't live up to the ideas I projected onto them. It's me. For misunderstanding who they were.

CHOOSING FAITH AND NOT FEAR

THE IMPROBABILITY OF
BREAKING YOUR LEG ON A BICYCLE

Circumstances do not make the man, they reveal him.

—JAMES ALLEN #worldchangerbook

Some people are faith machines. They are just sacred on top of sacred, bastions of credibility and perspective. It's like their bodies instinctively breed positive emotions, as if optimism runs through their veins. They seem to be naturally in tune with the laws of the universe and uniquely predispositioned to surrendering control and embodying peace.

When we perceive some individual is marked by this kind of rare maturity and balance, we conclude that maybe their bodies do not manufacture the same emotions as the rest of us.

Perhaps they are naturally immune to worry.

Perhaps.

It can definitely seem like it.

But probably not, right?

I strongly suspect that these balanced and wise people have the same physical properties you and I do. After all, any of us can imagine the worst-case scenario in everything. Every time our kid gets on a bike, we can envision that he is going to break his leg. We can worry any time we take on a new responsibility at work that we'll fail and get fired. We can think every time a relationship hits a hitch that we're about to be abandoned or betrayed. We can think any time we make an investment, we'll go bankrupt.

Our brain has no shortage of doomsday scripts ready on cue!

But I suspect even though these wise people are working with the same genetics and similarly frightening circumstances that the wise among us have made an important realization: *The ability to imagine a threat doesn't make a threat real. Projecting the worst doesn't make the worst likely.*

Imagination and truth are two separate things. And one does not always follow the other.

Think about it. Rather than break a leg, my kid is actually much more likely to build years of memories riding bikes out in nature and never have to visit the ER. Many people ride bikes without breaking a leg. In fact, we probably know far more people who have ridden a bicycle *without* breaking a leg than we know people who broke their legs riding them. Even if we do know someone who broke a leg, it's more likely the exception than the norm!

How awful then to live our whole lives in fear of the exception. The improbable. How much quality of life and peace of mind—how many beautiful bike rides through the countryside—would we lose if at every crossroad of risk, our minds imagined only what could go wrong instead of what could go right!

NOTICE YOUR FEAR, THEN LEARN TO CHANGE IT

THE WOLF YOU FEED

Courage is not the absence of fear,
but rather the judgment that something
else is more important than fear.

—AMBROSE REDMOON #worldchangerbook

It can be difficult to accept that perhaps we could reduce our fears if we took hold of our imagination.

Well that may be true, we chronic worriers say. *But I've always been a pessimist. That's just how I'm wired.*

Really? Can this be true?

Who wired us this way? God? The same God we maintain is *good,* the one we believe loved us so much he sent his son to die? The one who desires fullness for all humans, the one who isn't willing that anyone should perish? That God?

Are you sure?

Well, perhaps wired isn't the right word. Perhaps it's that we're conditioned that way. Programmed.

Thank you so much for clarifying that it isn't that we were designed this way but that we've been misprogrammed. Well then, we must fire our current programmers and find new ones, don't you think? The ones we've been using just aren't doing us justice!

Now I do not deny that some of us may very well be conditioned to react pessimistically. That fear may indeed be our first gut impulse. It certainly is sometimes!

But why on earth would we choose to stick with that impulse if it brings us so much anxiety?

Choosing to be controlled or directed by an impulsive fear is illogical for anyone, but perhaps it is especially confounding regarding those of us who very literally call ourselves *people of faith*. *Believe*-ers! People who claim God has not given us the spirit of fear, but of power and of love and of *a sound mind*![1]

So how do we sift our way through all these overwhelming decisions? Decide if we are going to let our children participate in a sport that might harm them? Are we going to let our child be exposed to diverse groups of people? Are we going to stay inside, doors locked, security system in place? Will we work among people some might consider dangerous? Will we do relief work where poverty and crime are high?

May I suggest that you begin by consciously choosing to dismiss that initial impulse and make a different choice? That you bank on faith instead of fear?

Well, that is easier said than done, some might say.

Granted, this is no easy task! No one ever said that it was. But just because it is difficult doesn't mean that we shouldn't try.

Now that you know what your go-to response to fear looks like, you can prepare ahead of time some statement or action you will choose to employ when those trigger emotions arise. Just like you might take Tylenol at the first sign of a headache or pop in a lozenge at the first sign of a sore throat, you can have a readied response on hand to meet the first sign of fear.

Perhaps it looks like this: *As this panic swells in me, I will choose to dismiss it. I will refuse to think about it further. I will replace this fearful thought with a more faith-filled one, I will go find a book to read or a movie to watch. I will pray or read an encouraging Scripture. I will strike up a conversation with someone. I will go for a run, I will concentrate on a chore, I will do something good for someone else. I will acknowledge this fear, look it straight in the eye and know that it's there, and then I will walk away to show it that it does not have control of me. I will boldly assert that I have not given my life to fear but to faith.*

Go ahead, try it!

And in doing so, you will apply the wisdom of this slightly modified but memorable old Cherokee legend.

An elder is teaching a youngster about life when the boy admits he is torn between good and bad.

"It is like I have two wolves fighting inside of me," the young boy confesses. "One is evil. He brings worry and anxiety to me. He paralyzes me with fear and keeps me awake and scared at night."

"The other wolf is good," he continues, "he brings me comfort and stability. He accompanies me in purpose and when he is with me, I am at peace."

Looking up at his elder, the boy concludes with a question. "Which wolf do you think will win?"

The old Cherokee replies easily, without so much as pausing to blink: "The one you choose to feed."

THE ILLUSION OF CERTAINTY

THE MAN WHO WAS AFRAID
TO PAINT FOR A LIVING

✖

*I honestly think it is better to be a failure at something
you love than to be a success at something you hate.*

—GEORGE BURNS #worldchangerbook

Fear is at the top of the list of reasons why people don't pursue
their dreams.

I think I learned to recognize this by studying the example of my dad who, as he neared sixty, announced to my
brothers and me that he was making a job transition. *Perhaps
he's going to transition to a less demanding role,* I thought. *You
know, as he nears retirement.*

But his next statement quickly ruled this out.

"We're going to plant a new church," he said. "It will meet
in the Bedford library."

And there I had it. This sixty-year-old man was not winding down. He was going off to start completely over, to recruit
new people and find a temporary rental facility until he and
others could find a new piece of property and engage the tedious process of getting a church building erected there.

But he did not strike out to do so as a reckless daredevil.
His decision came from a much more well-reasoned place. It

came out of a firm grasp of the concept relayed in the following story.

A man has worked in his job for ten years.

His work is not particularly taxing, but it's boring and his boss is an absolute jerk. The company often expects him to work long hours to ensure they have the most profitable year possible and so all the execs, in turn, can earn a nice year-end bonus! After ten years of working for them, the company generously gives him a metal clock that will double as a paperweight for his desk, which has his name inscribed on it as if to suggest just how permanent his place in the company has become.

At night, the man goes home and paints. He uses watercolors, acrylics, oils, and loves them all.

He takes his painting supplies to the waterfront, and he drinks in nature. His brushstrokes gradually capture a beautiful landscape that he takes back to his house to store until the next art fair in which he will rent a booth and then sell it to make his family a little extra money.

One night when the man is telling his wife how monotonous and uninspiring his job is, she says, "Well for goodness' sake, if it is bringing so much bad to your life, why don't you just quit and paint for a living!"

"Well, I've considered it," he replies, "and wouldn't I love that! But it's just not practical. Painters cannot guarantee they will have buyers; there is no way of knowing whether they'll be able to generate enough income to get by. There is no guaranteed paycheck."

His wife nods as if this makes perfect sense and smiles that her husband is so disciplined and practical.

But you are not nodding, are you? Please tell me you see the logical fallacy in the husband's reasoning.

It is when he says, "Painters cannot guarantee they will have buyers; there is no guaranteed paycheck."

Well, he is right, some might say.

Yes, of course he is right! Of course there is no guaranteed paycheck in that. But it is not because what he's considering is painting. It is because there is no guaranteed paycheck. Period.

But is he unaware that corporations like his frequently make news headlines for downsizing and pink-slipping staff by the hundreds? Surely he knows this.

Surely he knows that if push comes to shove, that executive who has been pocketing those bonuses these last ten years is going to be fighting to save his own job, not necessarily the jobs of the others who work for him.

Oh and you imagine how awful that would feel, if in year eleven, this man is then unexpectedly laid off from his job? If he suddenly realizes what he mistook as certainty was not really certainty, that what he misunderstood to be a guaranteed paycheck is not guaranteed. And that now those ten years of boredom have produced no security at all for his future. That after all that monotony, he is sitting there staring at his monogrammed clock, unemployed, not knowing where the next dollar will come from just the same.

If I was going to live in such uncertainty either way, he might think, I might as well be doing something I was passionate about.

Exactly!

Now hear me on this. What I am not saying is quit your job and go chase any impulse you fancy. Not at all.

That could be a terrible thing to do.

What I'm saying is that whether you stay in a more conventional job or you pursue your wildest dream, there is no certainty in either. In whatever place you invest your life—a corporate payroll office attached to it or praying the art markets open for you as a freelancer—the world offers you no guarantees. That you must place your faith in God to supply all your needs.

And also what I'm saying is if fear of an uncertain paycheck was one of the things that was stopping you from pursuing your most passionate dreams, then you must cross that excuse off the list. And maybe, just maybe, your children, like me, will be able to one day look out at what used to be a cornfield or abandoned lot and see the fruit of your dreams—in my dad's case, two churches—standing there instead.

A PUSH BEYOND THE WAY WE'VE ALWAYS LOOKED AT THINGS

THE COW THAT NEEDS TO GO OFF THE CLIFF

---

*The more I want to get something done,
the less I call it work.*

—Richard Bach #worldchangerbook

Perhaps now that you've come to question whether you really have certainty where you are, you might benefit from a push via a story about a monk and his assistant.

While traveling together, the two were taken in by a family who lived in a humble shack in the middle of nowhere. The family prepared a simple meal of fresh milk, cream, and cheese.

The monk was moved by their generosity and asked how they came by such good food while living in such poverty. "We have a cow," the father explained. "We drink her milk and eat her cheese and cream and sell what we do not need to neighbors who don't live too far away."

The next morning, as the two departed, the monk instructed his assistant, "Go push their cow off a cliff."

Sadly, the obedient assistant followed the orders of the monk, even though he himself was appalled by the act.

Some years later, the assistant was traveling through the

same area where he and the monk had taken lodging with the family in their little shack long ago. Overcome with remorse, the assistant decided to stop at the shack and repent of what he'd done. But unfortunately, as he searched up and down the road, he could not find it. Finally, he stopped at an enormous mansion surrounded by a manicured lawn, which he judged to be near the location of the former shack.

"Do you happen to know what happened to the family who used to live in the shack near here?" the assistant asked.

The owner of the mansion laughed. "That is us! We used to have that shack. But one day our cow fell off a cliff and in order to survive, we had to start doing other things and acquire new skills to make our way. We had to imagine new ways of doing things and take risks to forge out to accomplish them."

The assistant could barely believe what he was hearing, but the owner of the mansion was insistent. "I'm telling you," he said, "the day we lost that cow is the day that changed our lives."

I'll add only this: perhaps you too could stand to spare a cow.

PREPARE THE HORSE FOR BATTLE, BUT KNOW THE BATTLE BELONGS TO GOD

ROME FELL AND THESE COLORS COULD RUN

✕

You have to accept whatever comes and the only important thing is that you meet it with courage and with the best you have to give.

—ELEANOR ROOSEVELT #worldchangerbook

The ancient Roman Empire fell.

You probably heard.

But while we're talking about faith and fear and such things, I thought maybe I should put that out there as a reminder.

As part of a disaster relief team to Ground Zero after the 9/11 attacks, Rome's demise kept going through my head.

Not because of some penchant for pessimism or because of the destruction and carnage, although that was enough to give a person deep pause. But because among the dusty air and littered New York streets, next to the *Missing* posters taped up by those who searched for loved ones who'd been trapped in the towers, another kind of flier began emerging.

These colors don't run, the new posters declared. And

they sported valiant eagles with bold eyes and aggressively positioned claws with flashes of red, white, and blue, and stars and stripes, dancing in the background.

I've seen bumper stickers that said the same thing. *These colors don't run.*

And it had never before given me cause for reflection.

I'd accepted it.

Maybe even allowed for a fleeting feeling of world superiority. A short-lived moment of faith and certainty in my country. The guarantee of a good life growing out of the American Dream.

But then I was not looking at the remains of a World Trade Center tower either.

Now I watched firefighters climb through the wreckage of the building in the rain, heard generators power lights to keep the rescue efforts going, gazed into hopeless faces who waited in vain for more survivors to recover, and I knew something more deeply about whether a person should believe their country or their military or their government could provide such certainty that they would never have to run.

And here is my conclusion: *These colors would run.*

With no disregard to our nation's brave military, of which my father and grandfathers were a part, as I stood there wearing my dad's dog tags around my neck at the site, I knew in the place where one knows the deepest truths of life, that *these colors would run.*

That if ever we were not the superpower, if we did not have the sharpest weapon technology, the biggest missiles; if we did not have the intelligence to suspect our weaknesses, if we were taken off guard, if a force bigger and more prepared than us was upon us before we knew it, and we were there trying not to lose those we loved in the masses who fled away from the carnage . . . *we would run.*

The world has proven itself again and again to be capable of such catastrophic evils against even society's most vulnerable. Many times it has delivered the sort of darkness that has made even the strongest flee for their lives.

Admitting this aloud is a bit disconcerting at first perhaps. It is not often we pause to think that no nation, even ours, which is often hailed as being founded on such commendable principles, is impervious to being wounded or worse, destroyed.

Perhaps our rational minds don't know how to process the horror of this thought, to acknowledge the possibility that even the strongest things we know can be defeated. Perhaps this realization makes us want to throw our hands up and say, *Then why even have a government! Why even build a country or invest in a military! If none of these things bring us certainty, then why are we wasting our time?*

This is the sort of thought sequence that went through my mind as I stood in one of America's greatest cities, watching the aftermath of an unexpected crime against our nation.

But slowly, a bit of wisdom came alongside my thoughts as well, and I remembered a principle I had heard my dad stress many times, which he drew from the writings of Solomon.

We do the best we can to act wisely, my dad would say. We try to pursue good and stand against evil while erecting as many safeguards as we can and laying the groundwork for as much peace as possible.

Yes, some days, we will even prepare our horses for battle.

But: our trust is not in those horses.

We prepare our horses for battle, then, but we remember the victory belongs to the Lord.[2]

And whenever I think back to Solomon's assertion here, I am reminded too that Solomon, like me, likely learned this idea from his father, David, who similarly declared in Psalm 20:7, "Some trust in chariots and some in horses, but we trust in the name of the Lord our God."

And this is why I will not tell you today, nor will I teach my children, that our best hopes lie in whatever represents Rome to us today.

RESOLVE TO ACCEPT WHATEVER GOD WANTS TO GIVE

ANY STAGE YOU PUT IN FRONT OF ME

---✖---

We must be willing to let go of the life we have planned so as to have the life that is waiting for us.

—E. M. FORSTER #worldchangerbook

Did you know that the Bible gives us the exact prayer to pray over our dreams and passions and causes?

And no, I'm not talking about the prosperity gospel; of praying God will expand your projects' boundaries, increase your paycheck, and build you summer and winter homes with matching SUVs in the driveways.

I don't discount the right to pray for untold blessing, for making any number of lists—the best, hottest, richest, most popular. I'm just suggesting that Jesus modeled something different.

I had to think about this a great deal when my first book came out. To think about what hopes I should have for it, what sort of exposure or readership I should aim to build.

There are all kinds of books about such subjects. About promoting your book, marketing yourself, or building your personal brand. And I bought quite a few of them. Unfortunately, though, I could never get them to sit well with my understanding of Psalm 37, which I explained in more detail in this book's essay "Desires of Your Heart."

And so, after much thought, I arrived at a different prayer than the Prayer of Jabez or some similar book might suggest, which I scribbled into my journal back in 2005:

> God, I trust the outcome of this book—just as I trust the outcome of my life—to you. Whatever you do with either, I will try my best to cooperate.
>
> Whatever opportunity you put in front of me, big or small, I will take it.
>
> Whatever door you open in front of me, whether it is seemingly insignificant or intimidating and enormous, I pledge to have the faith to walk through it and to then find contentment in what lies beyond it.
>
> Whatever stage you give me the chance to step up on, God, I vow to take it. Whether that be a stage where I would tremble to stand at some world summit in front of thousands of leaders or on the stage of my living room where I might kneel in my bare feet to serve my future children.
>
> I accept that the biggest thing happening here is not a book being published but a life being grown. That this project more than anything else develops my faith, serving almost as a spiritual discipline that forces me to wrestle the hottest things in my soul to expression and to do it with enough wisdom that I will not later regret having done it. That it serves, in some small way, to make me one step more like Jesus.
>
> I realize that if I write this purely to capture what you stir in me, as some small move of obedience, that it will

have been undebatably well worth it. And that if you then allow it to influence others, that this will not be a requirement or something I'm entitled to but the icing on the cake.

With all of this said, then, I pledge to work hard to be a good steward of the learnings I believe you've allowed for me. But I also vow to never suspect that by some magic marketing or mythological prayer, I can catapult myself into greatness. I even acknowledge that I might not be qualified to judge what is or isn't good for myself or the masses.

As I've occasionally found myself in some conversations about success, where people have asked me about my expectations for my book and whether or not it played out as I anticipated, I have sometimes described this prayer. And a couple of times, the person listening has suggested that my faith is weak. That if I want to be used of God, I should name that. That I should shout it from the mountaintops and demonstrate I have the faith that he will do it.

But I have to humbly disagree about the usefulness of that kind of approach.

Perhaps that prayer, if spoken by someone else, would express exactly the spirit God wanted for them. Perhaps it would cast off timidity and usher in faith and prove very pleasing to God. For them, perhaps being willing to be used for greatness is a deeper surrender than what they've offered God so far.

But for me, with my own arrogance and perpetual belief that I am always right, that prayer doesn't serve my own growth or state of heart. For me, it would be no act of faith to tell God I would be happy to be widely applauded and to have my work universally gratified. We'd all like that. To say that demonstrates no allegiance to anything greater than ourselves. For me, the prayer that indicates a deeper surrender than what I had offered before was the one that volunteered to be servant. The one that concludes even though, on a lot of days, I think my own ideas are pretty brilliant, that if Jesus prayed not my will, but yours be done,[3] who am I to pray otherwise?

Instead, I choose to pray from the prayer God gave his followers, which is suited to speak over all our passions and causes and dreams:

"Your kingdom come, your will be done on earth as it is in heaven."[4]

A FEW IDEAS
ABOUT GROWING OLDER

AGING AS A SPIRITUAL DISCIPLINE

———————⬛———————

While I thought that I was learning how to live,
I have been learning how to die.

—LEONARDO DA VINCI #worldchangerbook

I think about loss and death a lot.

I don't know if everyone does.

Mostly, we probably try to shove such concepts out of our heads because it is just too painful to spend much time acknowledging that either we are going to die and leave everyone we love or everyone we love is going to die and leave us.

Even with the promise of reunion in eternity, it can seem like a pretty terrible inevitability all in all.

But it's true of course. For those of us who choose to notice, every day is a reminder we are aging. And there's no sense pretending that age does not advance us toward death.

There is evidence of this unavoidable reality everywhere, isn't there?

Each day brings a new smile line or gray hair.

Every birthday brings more candles on the cake.

Every year, our parents or our siblings or our friends look a little older than they did before. Even Hollywood stars suddenly go from heartthrob to fragile. And then every so often, the news alerts us that some athlete or actor who we looked up to in our younger days has died—and a bit of nostalgia floods over us as a small fraction of the world we called ours fades away before us.

All the while, the number of years on the invitation to our class reunions seem to jump overnight. We realize we've spent more days as an adult than as a child. That our new house or job or car is now far from new. And perhaps both sweetest and hardest of all, that our children who were infants yesterday have struck out on their own and are now having their own children.

And so, with each funeral or obituary, we grapple with the strangeness of this all. That we and others can be so alive, so full of vitality one moment, and cease to be present here on earth the next.

In the church, of course, we have the great hope—the hope of being absent with the body, meaning we are present with the Lord.[5] And we must muster up faith to hold this dearly, to bear it deeply within our souls among our most unshakeable truths.

But even this beautiful, transcendent statement can fall trite in days of grief. And the complexities and unknowns surrounding it can outpace our brightest philosophers and most sacred believers, leaving people like you and me looking for approaches that free our minds of panicked reflections and create space that is more conducive for our glorious hope.

Along these lines, here are a few ideas that come back to me and that help me find both passion and surrender as I proceed to my own transition to eternity.

The first is this: Worrying over pending death doesn't change it or slow it down. And dwelling on previous deaths doesn't bring people back.

This acknowledgment of what lies outside of our control prompts resolve that it makes no sense to obsess about death while we are still yet alive. It suggests that to devote too much alive-time to the subject of death is to let death prematurely rob us. It is to give up some bits of life to death before it has come.

Another is to experience the signs of aging with gratitude. To try to take each line that appears on our face as a reason to be glad that we have smiled so often. To reflect over our grandfatherly gray hair how, if we had not aged, we would not have experienced the profound gift of our grandchildren. To own how a life without age would have left us lacking as well, how if we had stayed as we were at ten or at fifteen or at twenty-five, it's very likely we would not have experienced life fully or that we even might've experienced life miserably. That the added years and the maturity and perspective that came with them are what kindly shaped our lives into a more valuable masterpiece than it once was. That aging, when done well, can be what invites the deepest quality of life we've yet to experience, so that it could be genuinely true—even at eighty or ninety—that we see the world so clearly that our very best ability to experience life as it was intended is just now dawning.

And the last idea I try to absorb is to see the deterioration of my body as a reminder that with each ability or sense that diminishes, with each ache or pain that surfaces, I gain more awareness and clarity of my human position and in its limits than I ever had in my youth. I fully see what I have always known, but never fully internalized: that I am not invincible. That with each day, I am becoming more dependent on others and on God, that I am coming out of self and selfishness into the greatest reliance on others and my Creator than I was ever able to previously achieve.

In this journey, I suspect, we will reach a kind of certainty that can only be experienced: that we cannot save ourselves. That we must count on God for each breath that forms in our nostrils, for each morning we continue to wake up, for each moment of sharp intellect and awareness we are able to hold on to. From that vantage point, looking back, I suspect we will realize it has been this way the whole time, but only then does it become so apparent.

And in this, I will be led to a place of absolute surrender. A place where I can, and will, have no choice but to finally give up my body and my health because my body and my health will be no trophies worth keeping. Yes, they will make the decision easier by giving up on me.

As all of this happens, I suspect I will be able to look in the mirror at the great-grandmotherly version of myself and be shocked at the outward manifestation of what is me. *Who is this person looking back at me with such a worn face and gray hair?* I can say to myself, *I am vibrant and alive! This is not me!*

And in this sort of moment, we will realize most fully that who we were was always much more and much deeper than the reflection we identified with all this time. That the shell my loved ones will place in a casket and bury in the ground is, joyfully, not me either.

And in this state, our soul will be as redeemed as it has ever been, which makes it the most readied it has ever been to find out what lies beyond. And perhaps, in this transformation, we will begin to catch a faint glimpse that makes us see how existence accomplishes a magnificent transformation. And perhaps this transformation will be so great that it will make us nearly certain that eternity can only extend this transformation to greater degrees. And in considering this, that there could be yet even more, we will reach a level of quiet awe that allows us some hint at how the apostle Paul was able to say those words we take great hope in: Death is swallowed up in victory. O death, where is your victory? O death, where is your sting?[6]

HUMILITY & PERSPECTIVE

A neighbor is a far better and
cheaper alternative to government services.
—JENNIFER PAHLKA #worldchangerbook

FAITHFUL IN THE LITTLE THINGS

TWO MEN AND TWO PACKS OF NAILS

The man who removes a mountain
begins by carrying away small stones.
—CHINESE PROVERB #worldchangerbook

Two men dreamed of doing great things one day. They woke up every day, longing to be anything but normal, anticipating the heroics that would one day be theirs.

They would bring people to faith! End homelessness! Find families for every orphan! They would see disease prevented and cured and set slaves free!

One day, after many days of waiting, they each received an unexpected, sparsely labeled package in the mail.

In the smallest, most ordinary manila envelope either man had ever seen, between some tissue and packing peanuts, lay a dozen carpentry nails.

Both men, of course, not having expected such a package, were immediately confused. Someone has sent us the wrong thing. Or they've sent us something meant for someone else. But who was the sender?

Both had similar thoughts. If someone is going to mail me surprise shipments, let it be gold I can sell for my mission. Let it be the deed to a building where I can set up shop for my cause. Let it be the key to a vehicle that lets me get on my way. Gold could pay to feed children, a building could house orphans, a bus could take underresourced children to tutoring or maybe to camp.

But a handful of nails? This is the most boring package I've ever received.

There aren't enough nails to build a building, not even enough nails to build a doghouse. Perhaps I could build a TV stand, but I have no time for TV. Can't the world see I'm meant for bigger things?

The first man tossed the envelope of nails out his window, into the junk collecting on the abandoned lot that sat next to his house. They clattered against the building and lay on the broken sidewalk between three rubber bands, a half-empty lighter, and some discarded PVC pipe.

The other man didn't want the nails either. He found them no more exciting than the first man had.

But he thought, *Well, since I have some nails, I should probably use them. I have nothing better to do while I wait for my adventure to begin.*

So he took four nails and a piece of scrap wood and he put up a little tree stand in his front yard, a low-lying seat for his children and the other neighborhood kids to sit in to shade themselves, to pretend to be lookouts in a high tower, over the summer.

But then, he got worried, what if a kid fell out of the tree? So he took six more nails and he put together a little makeshift stool to sit on, so he could perch on his porch and keep an eye on them.

Over time, so many kids started gathering, and he got to know them. And since he had nothing better to do, he began putting together activities for them. Things to keep them busy. Constructive things. Little things at first. Just until their parents returned from work.

They raked leaves and studied bugs. They hosted a lemonade stand. They competed to see who could throw rocks closest to a post. It was all little stuff, but they loved it. And their parents loved it too.

But then summer ended and the kids could not play outdoors all day. So they whined they were bored, until one day one parent came knocking on the man's door.

"I'm a lawyer," he said. "And I have an office building that isn't entirely used. What if I let you use one of the rooms to do your activities with the children in the winter?"

The man thought this was a brilliant idea. He began meeting with the kids of the neighborhood until the room could hold no more. Then others in the community began to pitch in to give these kids a place to hang out. And so gradually, a Realtor in the community talked to a member of the city council. They worked out a plan—through this man's own resources, donations, and free labor from area businesses—to rehab an abandoned building to be the new community youth center.

In the youth center, the man had a brightly painted new office with a desk and a picture window overlooking the community. And it was there that he decided to use his very last unused nails, the eleventh and twelfth that had arrived in his mailbox that day long ago. One he used to hang a photo of his toddler son and the neighborhood kids sitting in the tree stand, and one he used to hammer a little welcome sign onto the front door of the center.

It was the funniest thing too. As he pounded that welcome sign into the door, as neighbors looked on, he saw the most familiar sight. A tiny manila envelope full of twelve nails lay there next to the building, on the broken sidewalk between three rubber bands, a half-empty lighter, and some discarded PVC pipe.

"Oh I threw that out there many years ago," one neighbor spoke up, looking on. "Someone sent it to me by mistake and I had no use for it."

"Well, thank you," the second man said. "This is exactly what I need to build my second youth center."

* * *

You see why this story is important, I'm sure.

Perhaps you are fighting for your chance at greatness. For your shot to take the world by storm.

You have the heart of a lion, the courage of a warrior. Good intentions pump through your veins. You are ready to charge into battle, hammer down opposition, claim your prize.

You can already piece together how your actions this day, combined with future actions from yourself and others, could start the ball rolling to one day change the world.

The one small catch being right now you're unemployed and living in your parents' basement. Or you've been working for twenty years in a dead-end job and don't have a nickel to your name. You have no experience in the field you'd like to go in to. Or you've done some training or gone to college, you've got a great idea, but you're invisible.

The world has absolutely no idea who you are.

No publishers are bidding for your work. No music producers are calling. No movie or TV producers are trying to thrust fame or platform upon you.

Your great big ideas are just sitting there scrolled into your notebook, waiting for greatness to claim them.

But here is what you must know!

Big opportunities rarely arrive at your doorstep in their full glory. Huge prospects don't come that way, any more than babies arrive into the world six feet tall, walking, talking, and fully dressed to become president.

Quite the opposite. Most big opportunities arrive in small boxes. Thus your big dream isn't on hold. It's there right in front of you.

If your boss doesn't understand your vision and the organization you work for won't chase your dreams, then you may be ceilinged in.

So do something you can do. Something that is within your ability to control.

Strike out to do something else.

If you have no money, start a website.

If you can't write a book, write a letter.

If you can't sell your resources, then give them away for free.

This is exactly the thing that led to my first book, which has now led to four books after that.

Small acts may become the stepping-stones on your path to greatness.

Yours is not to figure out what those nails might become. Yours is to pound the nails you have and see what happens.

THERE ARE NO MONSTERS IN THE CLOSET

THE VILLAIN MAKER IS YOU

The only people who find what they are looking for in life are the fault finders.

—FOSTER'S LAW #worldchangerbook

They say the two most common fears are public speaking and death.

You know what never gets mentioned anywhere on the list, but I think we should be afraid of? What could also destroy our lives?

Our own imaginations.

Seriously.

Our own ability to concoct false hypotheses, to write fiction over the actual plots of our lives. To invent monsters in our closets that aren't really there.

Someone rubs us the wrong way. Probably more than once.

Let's call the offender Layla.

So maybe the first time we get into some sort of minor tension with Layla, we leave scratching our heads, wondering what caused the friction between us.

But after a couple less than ideal interactions, where Layla says or does something that annoys us, we take on the case like a detective.

We take Incident A and we string it to Incident B and Incident C, forming a hypothesis.

Layla doesn't value relationships, we theorize.

In Incident A, when Layla forgot to get the copier fixed as she'd promised, she clearly demonstrated how she doesn't really care about her fellow staff.

In Incident B, where she was short and a bit curt in a passing hallway conversation, she was obviously sending a message that she didn't have time for me.

In Incident C, when Layla skipped out on the bridal shower for another coworker, she suggested once again that relationships are not her priority.

Now, here is what we do.

We take the hypothesis back to work with us and we wear it, like a horse's blinders, filtering out all of Layla's peripheral good qualities and homing in on the parts of her we don't like.

Layla abruptly interrupts the coworker who confronts her about a job process that isn't working correctly? We note that!

Layla sends off a frank, one-line email to a friend who is going through a rough time? Write that down too.

The list goes on and on.

And we take all this data back to the lab where we dissect it and of course conclude our hypothesis is correct!

Just as we suspected, Layla *doesn't* value relationships.

How clever we are!

And how justified we are in writing Layla off.

Layla is an emotional monster.

But here is the problem.

We *may*, in all our hypothesizing, have sewn together completely unrelated circumstances.

We have not, for example, considered other possibilities.

Perhaps when Layla failed to fix the copier, she simply forgot about it. Maybe she would be mortified if her coworkers, who she admires and frequently talks about to her husband, were to point out her lapse in memory.

Maybe the day she was short in a passing conversation, she'd just locked her keys in the car or just received bad news.

What if she missed the bridal shower because someone in her family was ill or hospitalized? Because Layla herself is suffering quietly from chronic depression? Because she's in a financial crunch and couldn't afford a gift?

There's an ocean of possible explanations.

Maybe she interrupts her coworker because she doesn't have good conversational skills or is unaware of how she's breaching social etiquette. Maybe though she's even interrupting her coworker because she has no choice. Perhaps this coworker can talk away half the day and Layla is the one being dependable and attentive to work.

And so on.

Maybe, what actually happened is we speculated motives onto her that weren't indicative of her real character or heart.

Maybe we are the villain maker, not her.

THE LIE OF WHOLLY EVIL

WAR PROPAGANDA

———————— ✖ ————————

There is some good in the worst of us and some evil in the best of us. When we discover this, we are less prone to hate our enemies.

—MARTIN LUTHER KING JR. #worldchangerbook

Have you ever thought about shifting alliances?

No, I don't mean middle-schoolers who are best friends one day and worst enemies the next.

I'm talking about something larger. For example, in World War I, Italy fought with our side against the Central Powers. Italy was one of the good guys.

But by WWII, Italy was on the other side. War posters portrayed Italy among the villains.

So which is it? Was Italy wholly good, as in the First World War? Or wholly evil, as perceived in the Second?

Perhaps it was more likely the Italians of 1918 were not wholly good and the Italians in 1939 were not wholly evil. That in both 1919 and 1939, the Italians were like every other group of people: a mixture of good and bad. And among them, just as among Americans and residents of every other country, there were both greedy people and selfless people, both abusive people and compassionate people. And even within each individual, there were likely internal wars at work as well.

This, after all, is the nature of most humans.

The practice of "otherizing" people disturbs me more in the church than in any other facet of life.

I cannot tell you how many times I have been part of a conversation with friends on both the right and the left, who so willingly declare anyone two notches down the theologic.

To dis-identify with them completely, to take the actions of the most abusive and aggressive of another camp and use it as license to dismiss the value of all people who we perceive to be affiliated with them. To act as though everyone in that camp is wholly without merit, acting as if the positions on which they stand are the perspectives of those who have no intellect, no moral bearings, no sense of reason. That we alone have the answers!

To pretend, like old wartime propaganda, that an entire group is wholly evil. To push from our minds that within that group, despite their divergent beliefs, there may be morally centered, kind people who are genuinely attempting to sort the Scriptures in a way that honors the intentions of God. To forget that humans rarely manifest themselves as wholly evil or wholly good, that each of us is in process and therefore, a mix of both good and bad. To repress our knowledge that even among our "favored party," there is no one who is completely righteous. No, not one.[1]

I have been working hard to identify when I am tempted to unfairly otherize another group. And I have often found usefulness and humility in reframing the way I see people in the example contained in a story told about Francis of Assisi.

The story goes like this:

One day while Francis prayed, he reported being given

direction. God told him, Francis said, that if he wanted to know the will of God, he must give up all he was trying to possess and achieve and that when he did so, "all that formerly made you shudder will bring you sweetness . . ."

The thing that made Francis shudder was leprosy. He had been so averse to lepers, in fact, that he would not even look at them. Even if he donated alms for them, he would turn his head away and hold his nose.

But moved by what he felt was God's direction that day, when Francis went out riding, he met a leper. But rather than otherize this man, he conquered his revulsion by climbing down from his horse and intentionally forcing himself to kiss the diseased man's hand. The leper in return gave him the kiss of peace.

Of course, we all likely know the end of the story. That Francis devoted his entire life to the poor and socially discarded, even spurring an order of people who would follow in his footsteps.

How noble of Francis, we think!

That he set aside his distaste for the flaws of another human being who offended him and disciplined himself to act in love.

Yes, how noble of Francis indeed.

Now if only we respected his example, or the example of a Savior who did the same, to expose the "enemy others" we have slighted as the allowable exceptions of our otherwise Christian behavior, and we too made an effort to humanize them, to take down the propaganda, and kiss their hands with love in our hearts.

THE REAL HERESY IS IN WITHHOLDING GRACE

FALL FROM GRACE HEADLINES

---

*Millions of hells of sinners cannot
come near to exhaust infinite grace.*

—SAMUEL RUTHERFORD #worldchangerbook

I once did a study of headlines that included the term "grace" —not in the Bible but in news outlets.

The most popular phrase? *Fall. From. Grace.*

The expression was used in reference to all kinds of "news items":

A prime minister caught in a string of sex scandals
A Hollywood A-lister fighting ongoing drug addiction
Various sports teams on losing streaks
Companies whose stock has gone bad
A billionaire indicted for investment fraud
A superstar whose movie tanked
Our country's educational scores failing to compete
    with the scores of other industrialized nations
A corporation that filed for bankruptcy

Of course no one would argue that the basketball team whose shooting percentage dropped through the floor is the same sort of "fall from grace" as, say, the alcoholic who beats his kids in a drunken rage.

But it's not shocking that reporters are all over the map on what constitutes a "fall from grace." The general public tends to be pretty divided too.

We all know people who want to string up the guy who fails to replace the paper in the copier. But, still, we know others who want to let drunk drivers walk away from fatal accidents with just a slap on the wrist.

Lock us all in a room and we wouldn't come to a definitive statement about what qualifies as a fall from grace.

Which might be a kind of definitiveness in and of itself. Because maybe our phraseology is wrong and falling from "popularity" or "public approval" isn't the same thing as falling from grace at all.

Maybe what is most true is that actual grace is a whole lot deeper and bigger of a concept than whatever smutty stuff sells newspapers.

Maybe the phrase "fall from grace" is a big oxymoron because grace is . . . well, grace. And you can't fall out of grace any more than you flunk out of failure. The falling is an understood, built-in part of the idea.

Maybe grace defies definition and therefore, by nature, defies exclusion. And thus can't ever belong to or be reined in by any one person or group.

Maybe the real heresy isn't committed in failing miserably and earning the condemnation of the religious. Maybe the real heresy is acting like miserable failings fall outside of the grace of the God of that religion.

Maybe the greatest breaches of doctrine aren't always the

ones captured in bylaws and creeds and website belief statements. Maybe an equally grave breach of right belief is what is sometimes written into our behavior.

Maybe the real heresy is not branded onto the sinners but is instead attached to those who forget that even sinners love those who are easy to love.

Maybe one of the worst and most damaging misappropriations of the gospel is not failing to publicly feast on some other person's failure but is dismissing that Jesus said to love our enemies, to do good to them, to lend and expect nothing in return.

Maybe the greatest of the failings occur not when we throw lightning bolts at the fallen on God's behalf, but when we forget that our actions are a reflection—and sometimes a sad one—of a God who is kind to the ungrateful and the evil.

Maybe the real heresy is in failing to be merciful as our Father is merciful. [2]

In trying to reel back the gracious forgiveness Jesus extended to the adulterer or the thief on the cross or to those of us sinners who still exist today.

Maybe the real heresy is acting like our own behavior is so failure-free that we're qualified to do so.

A PRAYER FOR FUTURE FAILURES

THE PRAYER OF A WISE KING

---✕---

Success is not final, failure is not fatal.

—WINSTON CHURCHILL #worldchangerbook

I thought it appropriate if the final essay of this book that offers wisdom for world changers paid tribute to one of the world's wisest leaders.

And so I leave you with Solomon.

God, if you remember, offered Solomon anything he liked. But rather than asking for wealth or possessions or honor, Solomon asked for wisdom and knowledge to lead the people.[3]

He was mature like that.

In some areas of life, of course, we know Solomon went on to exercise great wisdom, while in other areas his lack of self-control and defiance of God's intentions led to both his and his country's demise.

So like most of us, he had his ups and downs.

But in all his reign, my favorite Solomon moment is the prayer he offered in 1 Kings 8 where Solomon is inviting God to inhabit the newly constructed temple.

It begins like this with an expression of gratitude:

Lord, the God of Israel, there is no God like you in heaven
above or on earth below—you who keep your covenant
of love with your servants who continue wholeheartedly
in your way. You have kept your promise to your servant
David my father; with your mouth you have promised
and with your hand you have fulfilled it—as it is today.[4]

Solomon goes on to say that they have finished the temple.
But he is not sure, he confesses, that God would even bring
himself to dwell with flawed humans.

And this is when the prayer becomes especially insightful
for me because it does not continue on solely in celebrating the
Grand Opening of the Temple or basking in their accomplishment in building it, but it begins to ask God—who may now
more formally dwell with humans—to forgive their shortcomings *in the future*:

"When your people Israel have been defeated by an enemy because they have sinned against you, and when they
turn back to you . . . then hear from heaven and forgive
the sin of your people . . ."[5]

"When the heavens are shut up and there is no rain because your people have sinned against you, and when they
pray toward this place and confess your name . . . hear from
heaven and forgive the sin of your servants . . ."[6]

"When famine or plague comes to the land, or blight
or mildew, locusts or grasshoppers, or when an enemy
besieges them in any of their cities . . . then hear from
heaven, your dwelling place. Forgive and act . . ."[7]

"When they sin against you—for there is no one who

does not sin—and you become angry with them and give
them over to the enemies, who take them captive to their
own lands, far away or near; and if they have a change of
heart in the land where they are held captive, and repent
and plead with you in the land of their captors and say,
'We have sinned . . . forgive your people, who have sinned
against you'; forgive all the offenses they have committed against you, and cause their captors to show them
mercy."[8]

I remember stumbling upon this prayer as a child and
being surprised because I had always believed prayers of forgiveness were for past acts, sins already committed.

But here, Solomon prays for God's mercy for their failings that had not yet come.

And this then was the inspiration for one of the prayers
I find myself revisiting again and again through life, one of
those prayers—like the ones I pray for my children—that I
offer countless times, both to underline my needs before God
and to focus my own heart.

I think of it as the Prayer of the Flawed, the cry of a person
both sinner and saint:

**God of Israel and God of those who follow you today, there
is no God like you who steadfastly stands by mankind through
generations . . .**

You have done well by me.

And I couldn't be more grateful.

**When I stray from your way of life, just as I have many
times before, please forgive me.**

When I temporarily get distracted from your purposes, ungratefully dismissing your hopes for me and temporarily misassigning my attention to something much lesser and more destructive, forgive me.

Please know that in my sanest moments my intention is to follow you closely and permanently.

That even though, in my worst moments, it may seem I have given my energy or affection to something other than you, that still—even in my flaws—the allegiance that runs deepest in me is to you.

That the rest of my life investments, good and bad, are a passing fad. That I will turn back from them and plead for your mercy. And when I do, I pray you will forgive me.

This is the truest and most enduring desire of my life: That when I am clear-minded, there is nothing I want more than to align myself to you, to be transformed by you. To internalize and embody your teachings.

So on the days where I fail to show that, please take confidence my heart will find humility, that I will be coming back to you with a saddened and repentant heart, and forgive me.

Mostly just know that no matter what my life brings in successes or failings, I am resolved to keep coming back to you.

AFTERWORD

Many times in my journey, both in my writing and in everyday communication, I have described how moved I have been at witnessing the passion Pastor Bill Hybels has for the cause closest to his heart, the work of the church.

"Give your life to this. Give all the money you can give. Give all the service you can give. Give all the prayers you can give. Give whatever you have to give, because for all eternity you'll look back over your shoulder and be glad you did.

"I can't count how many times I've fallen on my knees after a ministry event at Willow or elsewhere and said to God, 'Nothing else does this to me. Clearly I was born for this.'"

My prayer for all of us is that we will identify the things that God stirs inside of us, which burn bright white in our souls. That we will embrace the things we were born to do and give them everything we've got.

How wonderful that no one need
wait a single moment to improve the world.

—ANNE FRANK #worldchangerbook

INVITATION

I would love to invite you to share your passion for changing your part of the world with me.

If you send me your story in 500 words or less, I'll include it on my website at sarahcunningham.org. Just email it to sarahraymondcunningham@gmail.com.

NOTES

Section One: Worth & Success

1. Proverbs 14:23.
2. John 5:44.
3. Ephesians 3:20.
4. Luke 10:30–37.
5. Matthew 25:35–40.
6. http://catholiceducation.org/articles/abortion/ab0039.html.

Section Two: Health & Balance

1. Philippians 4:11–12.
2. Matthew 5:14–16.
3. 1 Thessalonians 5:21–22.
4. Philippians 4:4–7.

Section Three: Peace & Perseverance

1. 2 Chronicles 16:9; see also Psalm 33:18 and Proverbs 15:3.
2. www.namb.net/namb1cb2col.aspx?id=8590001104.
3. http://online.wsj.com/article/SB10000872396390443720204578004980476429190.html.
4. http://philanthropy.com/blogs/giveandtake/have-100000-nonprofit-groups-failed-in-the-recession/25952.
5. www.thefreedictionary.com/calibrate.
6. www.huffingtonpost.com/2011/10/05/steve-jobs-stanford-commencement-address_n_997301.html.
7. www.whatisorange.org.

8. Joshua 4.

9. Deuteronomy 6:8–9.

10. Ecclesiastes 3:1.

11. Luke 10:38–42.

12. Matthew 6:2–4.

13. Matthew 6:5–6.

14. John 12:4–7.

15. Luke 11:37–40.

16. Matthew 23:27–28.

Section Four: Risk & Control

1. http://www.theodore-roosevelt.com/trsorbonnespeech.html.

2. Matthew 7:1–5.

3. Mark 8:36.

4. Philippians 4:4, 8.

5. 1 Timothy 2:5.

6. 1 Corinthians 7:32–34.

Section Five: Alignment & Relationships

1. Philippians 2:4.

2. Gary Thomas expanded this concept in *Sacred Marriage*.

Section Six: Plans & Priorities

1. Genesis 1:28.

2. John 10:10.

3. Psalm 19:1.

4. Psalm 97:6.

5. Romans 1:20.

6. John 6:40.

7. Matthew 22:37–39.

8. Matthew 28:16–20.

9. 1 Thessalonians 5:18.

10. Romans 12:2.

11. Luke 6:46.

12. 2 Timothy 1:7.

13. Romans 12:1.

14. Matthew 5:9.

15. Romans 12:18.

16. Isaiah 5:20.

Section Seven: Passion & Identity

1. 1 Thessalonians 5:21.

Section Eight: Desires & Frustrations

1. Philippians 4:8.

Section Nine: Faith & Expectations

1. 2 Timothy 1:7.

2. Proverbs 21:31.

3. Matthew 26:39.

4. Matthew 6:10.

5. 2 Corinthians 5:8.

6. 1 Corinthians 15:54–57.

Section Ten: Humility & Perspective

1. Romans 3:10.

2. Luke 6:32–42.

3. 2 Chronicles 1:8–12.

4. 1 Kings 8:23–24.

5. 1 Kings 8:33–34.

6. 1 Kings 8:35–36.

7. 1 Kings 8:37, 39.

8. 1 Kings 8:46–47, 50.

SPECIAL THANKS

During five years of elementary and middle school, I attended a private school where—at the end of each year—teachers would assign each student a character award such as persuasiveness or perseverance.

I remember around 11, I asked my dad, "Dad, if I get 'responsibility' this year, will you let me babysit?"

My dad's response was this. "Maybe so. But I have no doubt you will eventually be responsible enough, what I hope for you is 'wisdom'."

I have to thank him for starting me on this journey, in which I've been collecting the words of the wise ever since.

All of the following books are also available as ebooks

THE POST-CHURCH CHRISTIAN

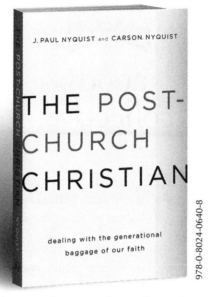

You've heard the stats by now: the Millennial generation is leaving the church.

Walking away in disillusionment and frustration, they are looking for new communities to welcome them. As they seek to follow Jesus, they are leaving the churches they grew up in to find a new way.

What will it look like as the two largest generations today intersect in leadership of the church?

MOODY
PUBLISHERS
www.MoodyPublishers.com

moody
collective

Moody Collective brings words of life to a generation seeking deeper faith. We are a part of Moody Publishers, representing this next generation of followers of Christ through books, blogs, essays, and more.

We seek to know, love, and serve the millennial generation with grace and humility. Each of our books is intended to challenge and encourage our readers as they pursue God. To learn more, visit our website, www.moodycollective.com.

MOODY
PUBLISHERS
www.MoodyPublishers.com

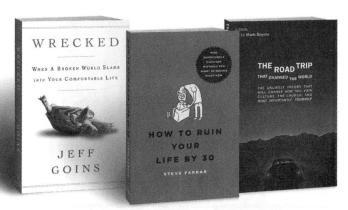

OTHER BOOKS BY
SARAH CUNNINGHAM

978-0-8024-0624-8

Inciting Incidents combines unique stories from eight creatives (artists, musicians, writers, thinkers, and leaders) managing the tensions between their faith, their place in life, and their work as artists. By capturing this next generation's battle between idealism and reality, these storytellers create understanding of those moments that truly shape us. Readers will be challenged to use their own art and their own life stories to find their way in God's Kingdom. The end result is that God has created each of us uniquely and we each have a growing part to play in His story.

MOODY
PUBLISHERS
www.MoodyPublishers.com

WRECKED

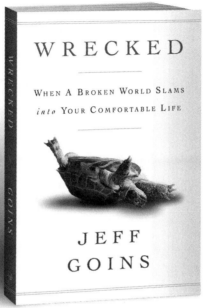

Wrecked is about the life we wish we lived.

It's a life of radical sacrifice and selfless service—and how we find it in the midst of suffering. Wrecked is a look at how we discover our life's purpose in the least likely of places: in the tough spots and amongst the broken-hearted. Wrecked is a manifesto for living like we mean it; it's a guide to growing up and giving your life away. This book is for us. A generation of young adults pursuing our life's work both responsibly and radically—how to live in the real-world tension of sacrificial living and the daily mundane.

MOODY
PUBLISHERS

www.MoodyPublishers.com